BUDDHISM

BUDDHISM

An Introduction to the Buddha's Life,
Teachings, and Practices

THE ESSENTIAL WISDOM LIBRARY

Joan Duncan Oliver

ST. MARTIN'S
ESSENTIALS
New York

www.stmartins.com

The Library of Congress Cataloging-in-Publication Data is available upon request.

ISBN 978-1-250-31368-3 (trade paperback)
ISBN 978-1-250-31369-0 (ebook)

Our books may be purchased in bulk for promotional, educational, or business use.
Please contact your local bookseller or the Macmillan Corporate and Premium Sales
Department at 1-800-221-7945, extension 5442, or by email at
MacmillanSpecialMarkets@macmillan.com.

First Edition: April 2019

D 10 9 8 7 6 5

FOR ALL SEEKERS OF WISDOM AND COMPASSION

Contents

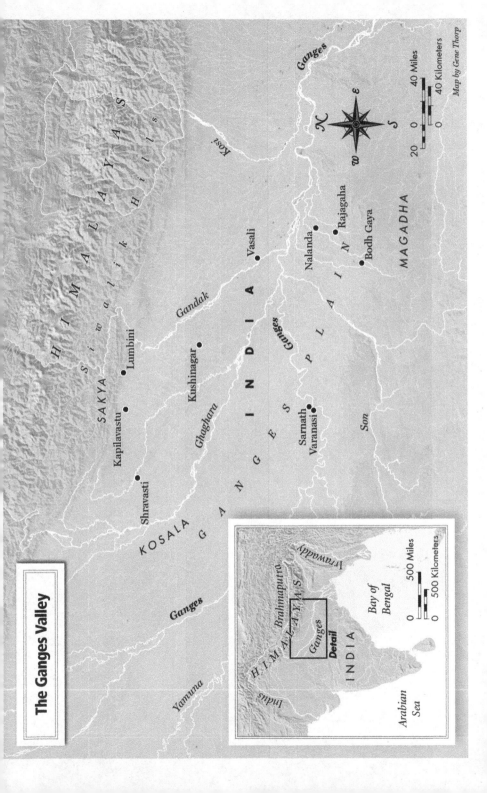

The Ganges Valley

HIMALAYAS

Siwalik Hills

Kosi

SAKYA

Lumbini

Kapilavastu

Shravasti

KOSALA

Kushinagar

Ghaghara

Gandak

INDIA

Vasali

GANGES PLAIN

Ganges

Nalanda

Rajagaha

Bodh Gaya

MAGADHA

Sarnath
Varanasi

Son

Ganges

Yamuna

Map by Gene Thorp

40 Miles

40 Kilometers

20

0

0

HIMALAYAS

Indus

Ganges

Brahmaputra

Irrawaddy

Detail

INDIA

Arabian Sea

Bay of Bengal

500 Miles

500 Kilometers

0

0

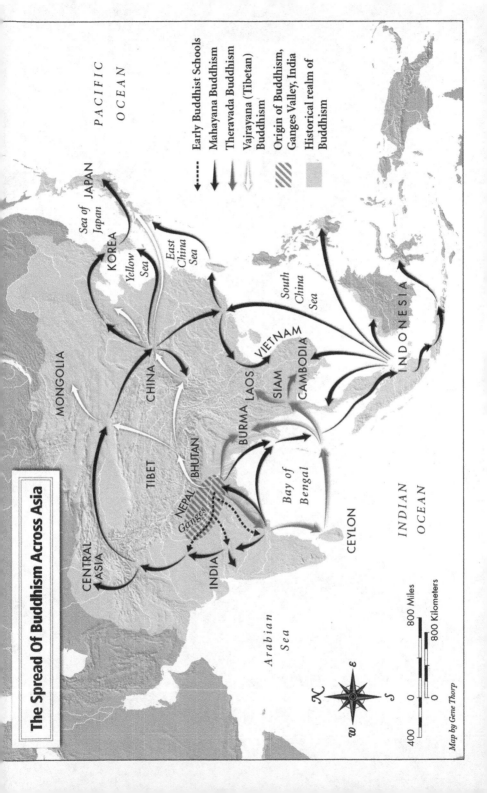

The Spread Of Buddhism Across Asia

Early Buddhist Schools
Mahayana Buddhism
Theravada Buddhism
Vajrayana (Tibetan) Buddhism

Origin of Buddhism, Ganges Valley, India

Historical realm of Buddhism

PACIFIC OCEAN

JAPAN
Sea of Japan
KOREA
Yellow Sea
East China Sea
MONGOLIA
CHINA
South China Sea
VIETNAM
CENTRAL ASIA
TIBET
BURMA LAOS
SIAM
CAMBODIA
INDONESIA
BHUTAN
NEPAL
Ganges
INDIA
Bay of Bengal
CEYLON
INDIAN OCEAN
Arabian Sea

N E S W

400
0
0
800 Miles
800 Kilometers

Map by Gene Thorp

Introduction

A book on Buddhism might more accurately be titled *Buddhisms,* plural. Buddhism is, in effect, many religions or, to some, not a religion at all but a philosophy and a way of life. All of these Buddhisms, however, stem from the same founder—Siddhartha Gautama, who came to be known as the Buddha, the Awakened One—and the same fundamental principles he taught 2,600 years ago.

One reason Buddhism has proved so adaptable is that the Buddha purposely installed no structure, no hierarchy, no leader to take over after his death. He left his teachings and the **Vinaya**—rules for the monks—and told his followers to work out their own salvation and disseminate the teachings as they saw fit.

What has happened over the centuries since might have surprised the Buddha. Some sources say he expected interest in his teachings to peter out after a few hundred years. Instead, the teachings took off and began their spread from India's Ganges

Valley across Asia and around the world. Wherever Buddhism landed, like water it took the shape of the container into which it was poured. In some places, it gradually absorbed elements of the local religion in classic syncretic fashion. In others, it landed whole cloth, as a new philosophy, and then was massaged by the locals into something more perfectly suited to their culture, temperament, and spiritual needs.

Like many Westerners, you may have been introduced to Buddhism through meditation. Mindfulness meditation is the new yoga, another ancient practice that has gone mainstream. As mindfulness reaches every corner of the culture, it is being celebrated as the key to reducing stress, optimizing performance, and building self-esteem. But Buddhism is all that and so much more. Perhaps you picked up *Buddhism: An Introduction to the Buddha's Life, Teachings, and Practices* to learn something about the origin of these techniques and the man who inspired them. Or perhaps you are wrestling with a painful loss or disappointment, and you're wondering if or how the Buddha's teachings might improve or even transform your life.

Before his great awakening, the Buddha was someone pretty much like many of us. He grew up in comfortable circumstances, not really focused on the deeper questions about life. Then, when he hit his early twenties, he began to have doubts about himself and what he saw happening around him. Even when life seemed to be going his way, he wasn't satisfied. *Why,* he wondered, *is there so much suffering in the world? Why doesn't happiness last?*

The Buddha wasn't the first to question the meaning of life or to wonder why it brings disappointment and pain. Nor was he the first to search for an answer. But he was determined to find a way out of suffering into true happiness—and when he found it, he spent the rest of his life teaching the way to others.

Today, nearly five hundred million people in the world consider themselves Buddhist. Not surprisingly, 95 percent of them live in Asia, where Buddhism is part of the spiritual tradition into which they were born. Here in the West, only about 1.1 percent of North Americans and 0.2 percent of Europeans identify as Buddhist. And only a fraction of those are "convert" Buddhists—people raised in some other spiritual tradition who have gravitated to Buddhadharma, the teachings of the Buddha.

For many people drawn to Buddhism, the attraction is what it's *not*. Unlike Christianity, Judaism, Islam, and Hinduism, Buddhism posits no God or supreme power, no everlasting soul, and there is no received wisdom, no priest class, no authority to supplicate or defer to, and for the most part, nothing to take on faith. The Buddha was an ordinary human being who liberated himself. He awakened to the truth of life and his own nature through a series of practices that any of us can try.

In the 2,600 years since the Buddha crisscrossed northern India, carrying the message that there is an end to suffering, different schools have developed within Buddhism, each with its own interpretation of his teachings and its own practices. But whatever form Buddhism takes, it retains the same fundamental view. "I teach one thing and one thing only," the Buddha said. "There is suffering and an end to suffering." We are not prisoners of our dissatisfaction, our disappointments, our desires, our losses, our obsession with self, he said. The method he laid out in the Noble Eightfold Path to enlightenment provides a practical way to transform our thinking from self-defeating to liberating.

What the Buddha taught is not theory or cant or wishful

thinking. He gave us a model and a method to awaken and then said, "Now it's up to you. Go for it!"

I knew none of this when I first encountered Buddhism many years ago. At the time all I wanted was to feel better—to be less anxious, more centered, happier about life. A friend suggested meditation and recommended Shobo-ji, a Zen center on the next block from my apartment. I had walked by the building countless times without ever noticing it. But there's an expression: *When the pupil is ready, the teacher appears.* So one Thursday evening, I took my friend's advice and attended the center's introduction to **zazen**, Zen meditation. Entering the **zendo**, the meditation hall, was like walking into another world—an oasis of calm in the midst of New York City. The minute I sat on the round black **zafu**, the meditation cushion, a whole new dimension of experience opened up, one that would change the direction of my life.

In the years since, I've studied with teachers in all three of the major branches of Buddhism—**Theravada**, **Mahayana**, and **Vajrayana**—and in **Bön**, Tibet's oldest spiritual tradition, which shares many elements with Vajrayana. My gratitude to the teachers and appreciation for the teachings and practices have only deepened over time, as I've experienced the transformative effect of the Buddha's legacy in my own life. My wish is that you too will find benefit in the wisdom and compassion of the Buddhist path.

How to Use This Book

Buddhism introduces you to the man we call the Buddha and to his teachings, as they have resonated through the ages and across the world. You will discover the fundamentals of what he taught and learn about core Buddhist practices you can try for yourself. The Buddha never claimed that any one method was suitable for all. He was renowned for "skillful means"—for knowing just the right teaching or practice to nudge each individual closer to enlightenment. But even then he encouraged questioning. "Don't just take my word that what I teach is the truth or that these methods are valid," he would say. "Try them for yourself and adopt only what you find to be true, only what works for you."

If the Buddha were here today, he would no doubt suggest that you keep that advice in mind as you read the following pages.

1

THE BUDDHA

Forget the teacher; remember the teachings was the Buddha's message to his followers. He opposed any cult of personality, any deification of him. Once a man saw him on the road and, struck by his clear eyes and vibrant presence, asked, "What are you? Are you a god?" "No," the Buddha told him. "I am awake."

The Buddha's great awakening is a model for spiritual seekers everywhere. He was a living example that it can be done—that the potential for enlightenment is within every human being and that we too can awaken to our true nature if we try. But who was the man behind the teachings? Before he became the Buddha, who was he? And what was the truth of existence that he found?

Unfortunately, neither the Buddha nor his **sangha**, his community of followers, left a detailed biography. And he lived eons before social media and confessional memoirs made everyone's life an open book. In fact, aside from some Vedic texts—ancient Hindu scriptures in Sanskrit—there were no written documents of any kind in India while the Buddha was alive. His teachings were strictly word of mouth, transcribed by his followers only centuries later.

The Buddha wasn't into personal revelations either. Enlightenment liberated him from self-concern, and he spoke about his past only when it was relevant to his teaching. Fortunately, however, for all he didn't say, the Buddha's life was sufficiently riveting for scholars and scribes in later times to embroider on myth, legend, and fragments of history to attempt to leave a biographical trail. Over the past millennia or two, creative minds have sought to make sense of the Buddha in poetry and prose, commenting on everything from his quotidian habits to his life-changing revelations. Given the embellishments through the years, aspects of his story are best appreciated for their symbolic rather than factual value.

The biography that follows is drawn first from the Buddha's own words as recorded in the **Pali Canon**, the collection of texts that represent the earliest record of his discourses. But it also gives a nod to more colorful renditions of the Buddha's life set down later on, among them the *Nidana-Katha*, or Jataka Tales, stories of the Buddha's previous lives; *The Buddhacarita*, or Acts of the Buddha, an epic biography by a first-century CE Indian Buddhist philosopher named Asvaghosa; and *The Lalita-vistara* or Play in Full, a third-century CE Mahayana Buddhist *sutra,* or text, recounting the Buddha's early days. By the time **Mahayana Buddhism,** the second major Buddhist tradition, came along, several centuries after the Buddha died, he had assumed transcendent status—quite a contrast to the altogether human Buddha of the Pali Canon.

Theravadan texts in the Pali Canon were rendered in Pali, an Indic dialect similar to what the Buddha is thought to have spoken, while the later Mahayana texts were in Sanskrit, a scholarly language common to ancient India and much of Southeast Asia. Except for material from the Pali Canon, most Buddhist terms in *Buddhism* will be in Sanskrit, a form more likely to be familiar to readers.

The Early Years

The Buddha's story begins in . . . well, even his birthdate is a guesstimate. Scholars have proposed dates ranging from 623 BCE to 322 BCE, but the current consensus puts the Buddha's birth at around 480 BCE and his death eighty years later, in 400 BCE.

He was born Siddhartha Gautama and raised in Kapilavastu, a city in the foothills of the Himalayas along the border of what is now Nepal. Northern India in those days was a checkerboard of independent states, ruled by tribes or clans. Siddhartha's father, King Suddhodana, was the raja, or ruler, of the Sakya clan. (After enlightenment, the Buddha was often referred to as Sakyamuni Buddha, "Sage of the Sakyas.")

Siddhartha's birth came at a time of great economic and social ferment in India, with the growth of towns and cities and an emerging merchant class. But the strict Hindu caste system was still intact. Priests and scholars—the **Brahmins**—comprised the highest caste, followed by the **Kshatriyas**, warriors and nobles like Siddhartha's family. Below that were the **Vaishya**—farmers and merchants—and then the **Shudra**, laborers. At the very bottom were the untouchables—not even worthy of being assigned a caste.

The Buddha would become one of the great spiritual revolutionaries of *all* time—an egalitarian who challenged the status quo and rejected discrimination of any kind. But as Siddhartha he was raised to be very much a man of *his* time. Suddhodana was a powerful and prosperous leader, and he brought up his son in princely fashion to inherit the kingdom. No luxury was spared. "I lived in . . . total refinement," the Buddha later said of his privileged childhood. "A white sunshade was held over me day and night, to protect me from cold, heat, dust, dirt, and dew." He had three palaces to live in: one each for winter, summer, and the rainy season.

The Buddha's legend begins even before his birth. If the story seems fantastical today, it merely reflects his world at the time, dominated by a Hindu cosmology richly populated with gods, goddesses, devas, and other protective and destructive otherworldly beings. The Jataka Tales give a detailed account of the Buddha's past lives as a **bodhisattva**, or Buddha-to-be, perfecting the **ten qualities** said to mark a Buddha—generosity, goodness, renunciation, wisdom, firmness, patience, truth, resolution, kindness, and equanimity.

In popular accounts of the birth, Queen Maya, Suddhodana's wife, had a dream in which a great white elephant descended from on high, pierced her side with his tusk, and entered her womb. The Brahmin priests who were summoned to interpret the dream said she would bear a son who would become either a **chakravartin**—a wheel-turner, or universal ruler—or a great spiritual teacher. When she was nearing her due date, the queen and her entourage stopped to rest at a park in Lumbini, not far from Kapilavastu. It is said that there, holding on to a flowering branch, she delivered her son. Legend has it that the future Buddha stood up, walked to each of the four directions, and declared, "I am supreme in the world. This is my last birth; henceforth there will be no rebirth for me." Rebirth is an alien concept to most Westerners today, but in the Buddha's time, it was a foregone conclusion, and spiritual practitioners strove for a favorable rebirth in one of the heavenly realms. The Buddha, however, was destined for *parinirvana*—a kind of super-enlightenment after which he would be gone forever, never to be reborn.

When Queen Maya returned to the palace with her son, more seers were called in to foretell the baby's future. Seven of them said that if he remained a householder, as laypersons were called, he would become a universal leader. The eighth, however, said he would be become a great spiritual teacher "and remove the veils of sin and ignorance from the world." Queen Maya and King Suddhodana named their son Siddhartha, "one who has accomplished a goal."

Queen Maya died a week after giving birth, so raising Siddhartha fell to her sister, Mahaprajapati, Suddhodana's other wife. Years later, Mahaprajapati would become the first nun among the Buddha's followers and a champion of women's rights in his sangha.

Ever mindful of the prophecy, Suddhodana was determined that his son would be a world ruler. He confined Siddhartha to the palace compound. The boy was a diligent student, and when Suddhodana thought it was time to make a leader of him,

Siddhartha easily mastered weaponry, horsemanship, and other manly arts. As he grew older, his father went to great lengths to ensure that nothing unpleasant crossed his path. Siddhartha's life was an endless round of sumptuous banquets and sensual pleasures, with musicians and beautiful courtesans attending to his every whim. The Buddha later described his youth as being a prisoner in a pleasure palace.

Suddhodana reasoned that marriage would keep his son on the world-ruler path, so he arranged a reception to introduce Siddhartha to prospective wives. Beautiful young women were paraded before the prince, who gave each one a bauble from the palace coffers. But when the last candidate, Yasodhara, stepped forward, all the jewels were gone. "Is there nothing for me?" she said, looking the prince straight in the eye. Smitten, he unclasped the emerald necklace from around his neck and fastened it around her waist.

As was the custom, Siddhartha had to prove himself as a warrior before Yasodhara's father would grant permission to marry his daughter. A tournament was arranged, with Siddhartha's cousin Devadatta and half-brother, Nanda, providing the competition. Though they were even more skilled than Siddhartha at archery, swordplay, and riding, Siddhartha miraculously outperformed them and won Yasodhara's hand. Perhaps Devadatta nursed a grudge: years later, jealous of the Buddha, he tried to kill him several times and take over leadership of the sangha.

Siddhartha and Yasodhara had a son, Rahula. Some sources say Rahula means "fetter"—and indeed family was one of the ties Siddhartha had to break in his journey toward self-realization.

For all the pampering, Siddhartha grew restless. Inevitably he became curious about life outside the palace walls. The encounters that opened him to the truth of suffering are symbolized by what are known as the **Four Sights**. After chafing at seclusion in the pleasure prison, Siddhartha persuaded his charioteer, Channa, to sneak him off to town. When Suddhodana got wind of the plan, he arranged for the roads to be swept of any disturbing sights. But the gods and devas—who interceded at key points throughout the Buddha's life—decided it was time to set his destiny in motion. As Siddhartha's chariot returned to the palace, a decrepit old man suddenly appeared beside the road. "What's that?" Siddhartha asked his charioteer. When he was told it was an old person and that aging came to all beings without exception, he was shocked. Twice more Siddhartha returned to town, encountering first illness and then death on succeeding visits. Haunted by the specter of old age, sickness, and death, Siddhartha agonized over how he could ever reign over beings who suffered so. How could he help anyone bear such sorrow and loss?

More likely, Siddhartha's encounters with reality took place over time, but once his innocence was pierced, his natural compassion emerged, and his quest for an end to suffering was ordained. The luxury of palace life no longer satisfied. On a fourth trip outside the palace, he encountered the fourth sight—a wandering ascetic, a **sadhu.** Suddenly it was clear to Siddhartha what he must do.

In one version of the story, Siddhartha informed his father that instead of being a warrior and a world leader, he wanted to become a homeless monk and search for an end to suffering.

It was not unusual back then for a man to leave home to pursue a spiritual path, but it was customary to wait until later in life, when he had fulfilled his familial and societal duties. Suddhodana tried to convince his son to wait, but Siddhartha had made up his mind. When he informed Yasodhara of his intentions, she was understandably furious that he would abandon her and their son.

In a more romantic version of the story, Siddhartha told no one of his plans but one night simply slipped away after sneaking a last look at his sleeping wife and infant son. He feared that if he woke them to say goodbye, he would lose the will to embark on his quest.

Accompanied by Channa, he rode his horse to the edge of the forest, where he cut off his hair and beard, then handed his sword and jewelry to Channa with instructions to give them to his father with the message that Siddhartha would not come back until he had achieved his goal. Serendipitously, a homeless monk appeared just then, and Siddhartha exchanged his princely garments for the monk's ocher robe and begging bowl.

At this point in some renditions of the tale, Mara—an otherworldly being known as the Tempter, the Evil One—arrived to try and dissuade Siddhartha. "Oh, come on, give up this silly quest and go back home," Mara urged. "If you do, in a week you'll be a chakravartin." We don't have to take Mara's existence literally to understand that he represented the unconscious pull of *samsara,* or worldly conditioning, that exerts power over the unenlightened mind. Well named the Lord of Illusion, Mara would return at critical points throughout the Buddha's life to test his resolve.

Going Forth

Renouncing ordinary life to become a wandering monk was known as "going forth." At that time in India's history it was becoming increasingly popular with the spiritually inclined who opposed the strict, top-down religion of the Brahmin priests. For Siddhartha, who was twenty-nine when he left palace life behind, going forth was the beginning of a hero's journey—a break with the familiar life he had known to search for something more authentic and enduring. Haunted by the suffering he had glimpsed, Siddhartha felt compelled to join other renunciates living rough in the forest. "It isn't easy, living in a home, to practice the holy life [that is] totally perfect, totally pure, a polished shell," he later said. Because he understood the challenges so well, he was supportive of his lay followers later on.

The monks spent their mornings making an "alms run" to a nearby town, where they relied on the generosity of the townspeople to fill their begging bowls with food. During one such run in the city of Rajagaha, the capital of Magadha, one of the great kingdoms of northern India at the time, Siddhartha was spotted by Bimbisara, the king. Recognizing Siddhartha as well born and of warrior stock, the king urged him to stay and lead the Magadhan army. But Siddhartha refused, saying he had renounced worldly life for a spiritual quest. Bimbisara respected his commitment and told Siddhartha, "When you find what you're looking for, come back and teach me." After enlightenment, the Buddha kept his promise, and King Bimbisara became a disciple and close friend of the Buddha's, as well as a generous benefactor.

Siddhartha next looked for a teacher. He went first to Alara Kalama, who taught the **jhanas**, ever-higher levels of meditative absorption. Siddhartha quickly attained the seventh level, direct knowledge of nothingness—boundless space. But he did not think Alara Kalama's methods would lead to enlightenment, the "sublime peace," so he moved on.

He next sought out Uddaka Ramaputta. Ramaputta had reached an even higher level of absorption, the dimension of neither perception nor non-perception, which Siddhartha soon attained. Ramaputta offered Siddhartha the opportunity to stay and teach alongside him, but Siddhartha knew this too would not lead to the supreme awakening he sought, so again he moved on.

He then joined up with five other wandering ascetics pursuing enlightenment. Believing that the path to realization lay in extreme self-mortification, they pushed themselves beyond physical limits. Siddhartha became so emaciated that his "spine stood out like a string of beads," he later said, and when he touched his stomach, he could feel his backbone underneath the skin.

Near death but no nearer awakening, Siddhartha was visited by his old nemesis, Mara. Unhappy that Siddhartha might achieve enlightenment and thereby escape his influence forever, Mara launched an all-out offensive to plant doubt in Siddhartha's mind. Mara's efforts only made Siddhartha more determined to succeed. But first he had to survive an onslaught of operatic proportions.

Poets and historians had a field day with Siddhartha's last stand against the Tempter. In his narrative poem *The Light of Asia*—a nineteenth-century romantic view of the Great Awakening—Sir Edwin Arnold pulled out all the stops in describing the monsters Mara unleashed on Siddhartha: "Wherefore there trooped from every deepest pit / The fiends who war with Wisdom and the Light." First Mara sent out his daughters, Discontent, Craving, and Desire, "and their crew / Of passions, horrors, ignorances, lusts," but their seductions failed to arouse Siddhartha. Then came the "ten chief Sins," including Doubt, who "Hissed in the Master's ear: 'All things are shows, / And vain the knowledge of their vanity; Though dost but chase the shadow of thyself; / Rise and go hence . . .'" Still Siddhartha sat unmoved.

Then Mara's "demon-armies" launched a barrage of gruesome weaponry, but those efforts too fell short. The shower of hot coals turned into a gentle rain of flowers. The snakes and snarling beasts cowered and withdrew. Boulders that Mara hurled stopped dead in midair. Through it all, Siddhartha sat firm. Furious, Mara stirred up a mighty whirlwind. "Give it up, Mara," Siddhartha told him. "I can no more be shaken by you than Mount Meru [a holy mountain] can be shaken by the wind."

Out of options, Mara bellowed, "Get up, Siddhartha! That seat belongs to me!" Siddhartha countered, "No, Mara, this seat belongs to me. It's where Buddhas-to-be sit on the day of their enlightenment. It's not you who has perfected himself for the good of all mankind."

Undaunted, Siddhartha challenged Mara, "Who's your witness to your compassion and generosity?"

Mara gestured to his army. "We're his witnesses! We're his witnesses!" they shouted in unison. "Who's *your* witness?" Mara asked.

"I have no human witness here with me now," Siddhartha replied. Then he reached down with his right hand and touched the ground. "Let the earth be my witness of all the help I've given in past lives." With that, there was a mighty rumbling—the earth acknowledging, "*I* am your witness."

Defeated at last, Mara slunk off.

Siddhartha settled back into meditation, but he was too weak to concentrate. *Starving myself hasn't worked,* he thought. *Perhaps there's a better way.* He recalled a day in childhood when he had accompanied his father to the fields. His nursemaid had parked him in the shade of a rose-apple tree while she went to watch the ploughing. Sitting cross-legged, Siddhartha had fallen into a blissful meditative state. He was still sitting like that hours later when his nursemaid returned. *Maybe,* Siddhartha thought as he remembered that day, *pleasant states aren't all detrimental to meditation; they might even be beneficial.* With that, he arrived at a **Middle Way** between the extremes of self-indulgence and self-denial. It became the defining principle of the Noble Eightfold Path to enlightenment that he later taught.

Just then, the legends say, a young girl wandered by and, seeing Siddhartha's sorry state, offered him some rice milk. Slowly, as he began to nourish himself over the next days, his body recovered and his mind grew sharp.

But when the five ascetics saw that Siddhartha had broken the fast, they figured he had given up the struggle. They abandoned him in disgust. Alone, Siddhartha sat under a fig tree and vowed not to move until he awakened. Today, a descendent of that fig—later named the **Bodhi tree,** or Buddha tree—stands on the spot of the Buddha's enlightenment, in the town of Bodh Gaya in northeast India, some 280 miles south of Kapilavastu, where he was raised.

Awakening

Culminating six years of intensive practice, the Buddha's great awakening is said to have taken place over one eventful night. In some versions of the tale, Mara's assault came not days before his awakening but during that very busy night. Whether we interpret the events literally or figuratively, in the end the Buddha's realization was profound.

During the first watch of the night (6:00 pm to 10:00 pm), when his mind was calm and clear, Siddhartha recalled in detail all of his past lives—"a hundred thousand births"—during which he had purified himself to come to earth and awaken as the Buddha, never to be reborn.

During the second watch of the night (10:00 pm to 2:00 am), Siddhartha was shown the workings of **karma**, the law of cause and effect. He saw beings of all kinds being reborn in the next life. Those whose conduct had been good went to the heavenly realms, while those whose conduct had been poor were consigned to the lower hell realms.

Then in the third watch of the night (2:00 am to 6:00 am), he gained knowledge of what he would later call the **Four Noble Truths**: the existence of suffering; the origin of suffering; the end to suffering; and the way out of suffering. He was released from the bonds of the **Three Poisons**—greed, anger, and delusion—the three unwholesome mental states that are the source of all human suffering and keep us cycling through samsara, lifetime after lifetime.

As the morning star arose, Siddhartha awoke to the truth of existence. Fully enlightened as the Buddha, he was freed from suffering and rebirth. Thereafter, he would be known as the **Tathagata**—the one who has gone and the one who has come. He was thirty-five years old.

After Enlightenment

For the next forty-nine days after his awakening, the Buddha stayed close to the Bodhi tree. During the first week, he was lost in the bliss of release. On the eighth day, he returned to his examination of karma, this time focusing on **dependent origination**, the chain of conditioning that binds us to suffering. First, he considered the progression of the twelve links in the chain. Then he considered the progression in reverse that breaks the chain of conditioning and ends the cycle of suffering.

The Buddha pondered whether he should teach what he had discovered to others. Probably not, he decided. This knowledge was deep, subtle, and hard to grasp. People were too attached to worldly pleasures to understand, so why bother?

Then the gods interceded. Brahma Sahampati—the most senior of the otherworldly beings in Buddha's day—lamented, "The world is lost! The world is destroyed!" The "Self-Awakened One" would rather live in ease than teach the **Dhamma,** he thought. [The Pali word *Dhamma* and its Sanskrit equivalent, *Dharma,* sometimes translated as "truth," refer to the Buddha's teachings.] Brahma implored the Buddha to reconsider: "There are beings with little dust in their eyes"—with fewer delusions about reality—"who are falling away because they do not hear the Dhamma," he said. "There will be those who will understand [it]."

Brahma's plea finally got through. The Buddha agreed to

teach. The question then was who would listen. His teachers, Alara Kalama and Uddaka Ramaputta, had recently died. Then he thought of the five ascetics from the forest. They were staying at the Deer Park near Varanasi, a hundred or so miles away.

The Buddha set off for the Deer Park. En route, he ran into another monk. The monk gave him the standard greeting between monastics, asking, "Who's your teacher?"

"No one," the Buddha replied. "I am self-awakened, all-knowing."

"Whatever," said the monk, shaking his head. "May it be so," he muttered as he hurried off.

Turning the Wheel of Dharma

As the Buddha neared the Deer Park, the five ascetics saw him in the distance. "Here comes Gautama, living the life of luxury," they said. "He doesn't deserve to have us bow to him." Still, when the Buddha arrived, they offered him a seat and called him "friend."

The Buddha corrected them. Not friend, but the Tathagata, he said. He had attained nirvana—enlightenment.

"But you gave up the quest for a life of luxury," the ascetics protested. "So how could you be enlightened?"

The Buddha assured them he hadn't been living luxuriously and told them about the Middle Way. When he offered to teach them what he had found, they demurred, still wary. But he was so calm and clear-eyed that finally they relented. In what later came to be known as the First Turning of the Wheel of Dharma, the Buddha explained the Middle Way, the Four Noble Truths, and the Noble Eightfold Path. The ascetics were so moved that one of them awakened on the spot.

The Buddha's second sermon was a teaching on *anatta,* or non-self. If we look for a permanently existing self, he explained, we discover that none exists. There is no eternal soul, no lasting, independent entity we can identify as *me.* This was a revolutionary idea that flew in the face of conventional wisdom, but the monks were receptive to it. When the Buddha finished speaking, the other four were enlightened.

The Teaching Years

From the Buddha and the five monks, the sangha grew exponentially. When it reached sixty monks, the Buddha told them to fan out around the countryside and spread the word. In no time, not only had more monks joined the sangha but the Buddha also had begun to attract a following among royalty, merchants, and even Brahmin priests.

Among the first lessons the monks were taught was etiquette, so they would know how to behave properly around people from all walks of life—in the sangha, in social gatherings, and on their alms runs. A monk endowed with seven qualities would be worthy of respect, of offerings, of hospitality, the Buddha said. What were those qualities? "A sense of Dhamma, a sense of meaning, a sense of himself, a sense of moderation, a sense of time, a sense of social gatherings, and a sense of distinctions among individuals."

Many of the Buddha's followers were surprised that he ignored social conventions like class. But he was adamantly opposed to the caste system and was as likely to welcome an untouchable or a prostitute as the nobles and merchants who became disciples. Ethical behavior is a core aspect of the Noble Eightfold Path, and on more than one occasion, a Brahmin who treated others as inferior was shown the error of his ways. Once, when the Buddha went to a Brahmin's house seeking alms, the homeowner assumed he was an outcast and refused to serve him. The Buddha calmly told the homeowner that it was those who lacked sympathy for their fellow human beings who were the real outcasts. Deeds, not birth, made one a Brahmin or an outcast, he said.

The sangha was open to all who sought the Dharma. In one famous instance, the Buddha welcomed a murderous robber, Angulimala, who had been terrorizing residents throughout the kingdom of Kosala, which included the Sakya territory the Buddha's father ruled. One day, the Buddha was walking alone when Angulimala spotted him coming down the road. *Mmm,* the robber thought. *This one's ripe for the picking.* As the Buddha drew near, Angulimala glowered at him menacingly and demanded, "Stop, monk!" The Buddha met his gaze and said calmly, "I *have* stopped. Why don't you?" When Angulimala asked what he meant by "stopped," the Buddha said that he had given up all violence. Angulimala was so overwhelmed by the Buddha's presence that he immediately joined the sangha. He became a model monk, but sadly, he never quite escaped his past. Sometimes the townspeople refused to give him alms. This was a teaching on karma, the Buddha gently reminded him.

The Buddha's way was to walk across India's Northern Plains from town to town with a group of monks and then set up camp nearby and offer teachings to the townspeople, many of whom gave alms to the monks or invited them to lunch. As the sangha grew, it became difficult to wander as a group, and during the rainy season, it was imperative to stay in one place. Wealthy followers gave the Buddha land and shelter for encampments. Once, one of the Buddha's primary benefactors, a merchant known as Anathapindika—"almsgiver to those without protection"—invited him to teach in Savatthi—the capital of Kosala, today named Shravasti—but a suitable place had to be found. A wealthy landowner, Prince Jeta, had a property nearby, but when Anathapindika approached him about buying it, the prince turned him down flatly, saying, "Not if you paved the land in gold!" Determined, Anathapindika went out and did just that, laying gold pieces across the entire park. Jeta was so impressed by Anathapindika's devotion that he erected a huge gate to the park and planted trees for the Buddha, then joined the sangha. Jeta's Grove was the site of many teachings and rainy-season retreats after that.

Another generous benefactor was King Bimbisara of Magadha, the ruler who had met Siddhartha when he first went forth. On hearing the Buddha teach, the king became a stream enterer—the first of the four progressive stages on the path to enlightenment. (The others are once-returner and non-returner—referring to rebirth—and finally, enlightened one, or *arahant* in Pali, *arhat* in Sanskrit.) Out of gratitude, Bimbisara gave the sangha the Bamboo Grove, where they spent many rainy seasons.

Bimbisara's brother-in-law, King Pasenadi of Kosala, figures in a number of the Buddha's discourses. On meeting the Buddha, Pasenadi questioned how someone so young could claim to be enlightened, when other honored teachers refused to make that claim. The Buddha replied that there were four things that should not be dismissed for being young: a warrior, a snake, a fire, and a monk. A warrior, a snake, or a fire, if improperly treated, could take your life, the Buddha said, and mistreating a monk would result in bad karma. So a wise person would always show those four respect.

Because so many of the Buddha's sermons were delivered to an audience of monks, it is often assumed he was really only interested in the monastic community. Not so. The Buddha was just as attentive to his lay disciples, who numbered in the thousands. Many of his discourses on subjects like business and conflict resolution were in response to questions from his lay followers. The Buddha established five precepts for laypersons and counseled householders on honoring their responsibilities regarding marriage and family.

The Buddha's own family kept tabs on him from the time he left the palace, and once the sangha was established, he agreed to return to Kapilavastu for a visit. On his arrival, Yasodhara told Rahula, who was seven years old by then, "That is your father. Go and ask him for your inheritance." The Buddha explained to his son that he had taken a vow of poverty and had no material wealth to give. What he could offer, however, was a treasure of far greater value—the Dharma. Later, as the Buddha was leaving to return to the monks, Rahula asked to go with him. Reluctantly, the family agreed. Rahula was placed under the care of the Buddha's head monks, Shariputra and Moggallana, serving as a novice monk until he received full ordination at age twenty. Yasodhara, meanwhile, had secluded herself in the palace as a renunciant—one who has given up worldly life—ever since Siddhartha had gone forth. Eventually, she too joined the community as a nun and became enlightened.

The Buddha's stepmother, Mahaprajapati, lobbied hard to be

ordained, but the Buddha repeatedly put her off, until, it is said, Ananda, the Buddha's cousin and later his devoted attendant, interceded, and Mahaprajapati became the first nun. The condition for ordaining women was a longer list of rules for the nuns than for the monks, largely for their own protection. The terms did not deter women from joining the order, however, including one of King Bimbisara's wives.

Old Age

The sangha continued to grow. But after twenty years of teaching, when the Buddha was fifty-five, he felt himself slowing down. He decided to make some changes. He reduced his travel schedule, staying longer in each place to teach. And he asked to have a permanent attendant, instead of the shifting parade of monks who had served him in the past. His cousin Ananda was named to the post, and for the next twenty-five years, Ananda remained at the Buddha's side, a model of devotion and dedication to the Buddha's welfare.

As the years went on, the community continued, but not without internal discord. The most serious threat came from the Buddha's cousin Devadatta, his childhood rival. Devadatta tried unsuccessfully to take over the sangha and made three failed attempts on the Buddha's life. In one, he unleashed a raging elephant that charged the Buddha. Ananda jumped in to be a shield. Like others of high spiritual attainment, the Buddha was said to possess superpowers known as **siddhis**, but he seldom displayed them except to convince doubters of the power of the Dharma. This time, however, he interceded and stopped the elephant in its tracks. Only then was Ananda willing to stand down.

With age came inevitable losses. His son Rahula had died years earlier, and one by one, the Buddha lost his closest friends and his trusted monks Shariputra and Moggallana. One day, as the Buddha was warming himself in the sun, Ananda commented on his stooped back and flabby, wrinkled legs. "That's the way it is, Ananda," the Buddha said. "When young, one is subject to aging; when healthy, subject to illness; when alive, subject to death."

The Final Days

In the last year of his life, as he was nearing eighty, the Buddha set out on a kind of "farewell tour." Crossing the Ganges Valley, he taught on key points of the Dharma and delivered his message of nonviolence in areas where conflict was threatening to break out. Everywhere he went, sangha members, whether kings and princes or householders and monks, rushed to pay homage to him. When the Buddha caught a deadly disease, Ananda had a meltdown, frantic about how he would live without the Buddha to guide him. Reminding him that even a Buddha's body is impermanent, the Buddha exhorted Ananda to soldier on.

After the Buddha rallied, Ananda was overjoyed. "I was beside myself with worry," he gushed. "But I was sure you wouldn't die without making practical arrangements about who would lead the sangha."

"What more does the community of monks expect of me?"

the Buddha asked. "I have taught them everything I know, everything they need to attain enlightenment." As for who would assume leadership of the sangha, that wasn't his concern, the Buddha said. The monks had the rules of the order, and as long as they continued to practice diligently, they would be fine. His advice was to let the Dharma be their guide. "Be islands unto yourselves, with the Dharma as your refuge, seeking no external refuge."

A few days later, while they were sitting together at a shrine, the Buddha told Ananda that anyone who, like the Tathagata, developed the four bases of power—concentration, persistence, intent, and discrimination—could "live out the age": live to one hundred if he wanted. But even when he repeated that two more times, Ananda failed to take the hint and urge him to live on.

Mara made one last pass at the Buddha. Reporting it later to Ananda, the Buddha said, "I told him to save his breath, that three months from now, the Tathagata would pass away. In this way, I let him know I had renounced the will to live on." Hearing this, Ananda exclaimed, "Oh, please don't go! Please don't go! Stay out of compassion for the world and the well-being and happiness of all!"

Too late, the Buddha thought. *You should have said something the other day when I told you that Buddhas could live to 100 if they wanted.* Instead, he merely said, "Enough, Ananda. Don't beg me again, for the time has passed for such an entreaty."

The end came one night after the Buddha ate a meal of tainted food. He had known it was spoiled but told Ananda not to mention it to his host. Instead, he said, "Come, Ananda, let us go to Kushinagar." When they arrived, he asked Ananda to prepare a bed between two fig trees with the head facing north. The Buddha stretched out on his right side with one foot on top of the other in the sleeping lion's pose—the position traditionally recommended for dying.

At that point, a follower begged to see the Buddha for a last blessing. Ananda tried to shoo him away, but the Buddha—generous to the end—waved the man forward. Then, with his monks gathered around him, the Buddha exhorted them: "All compounded things are impermanent, subject to decay. Strive on with diligence!"

With that, he progressed through the sequence of meditative states to parinirvana, never to return.

2

BUDDHISM AFTER
THE BUDDHA

It is not hard to imagine that after the Buddha's death, his followers wondered, *what now?* The Buddha had purposely named
no successor and left no formal structure. The monks had the
Vinaya, the rules of the order. And it was the teachings, not the
teacher, he had said, that would sustain the sangha. The monks
should practice diligently with the Dharma as their refuge and
work out sangha matters on their own.

About the Dharma, however, the Buddha was adamant: he
wanted it transmitted accurately. But back then, centuries before written texts were common in India, there was no official
record of the thousands of oral teachings by the Buddha and his
senior monks. So a few months after the Buddha's parinirvana,
Maha Kassapa, the sangha elder, is said to have convened a council of five hundred of the Buddha's most accomplished monks
to recite the teachings and training rules so they would not
be misrepresented or lost to future generations. Maha Kassapa
was to recite the training rules, and Ananda was the clear

choice to recite the teachings—the *suttas*, or discourses. Not only had he been the Buddha's devoted attendant for the last twenty-five years of the Buddha's life but he had an excellent memory. There was a slight hitch: unlike the other 499 monks, Ananda was not yet an arahant—a fully awakened one—and some said he should not participate. Hearing that, Ananda redoubled his efforts and attained enlightenment the night before the council began. Ananda's vast recall—and boundless heart—may be among the main reasons why so many of the Buddha's teachings survived.

The first Buddhist council agreed on doctrinal matters—the body of teachings and how they would be transmitted orally. A century or so after the Buddha died, a second council was convened to settle issues around the Vinaya. A group of monks called for an update of the rules. The discussion was fractious, and afterward the sangha divided. Ten thousand monks formed the Mahansanghika school, which spread across northern India, while the Staviras, followers of the original teachings, moved south. (Later, there were further divides, until by the third century CE, Buddhism had splintered into eighteen different schools.)

Emperor Ashoka is credited with giving Buddhism a needed boost in the third century BCE. One of India's great emperors, Ashoka was a hot-tempered warrior with a drive to conquer until one day, walking the battlefield after his war against the Kalingas, he was appalled by the terrible carnage. After that he became a patron of Buddhism, convening a third Buddhist council to deal with corruption in the sangha. Then Ashoka dispatched monks to spread Buddhism to Sri Lanka, central Asia, and as far away as Greece. He also built stupas—stone reliquaries—in the places the Buddha had identified before his death as pilgrimage sites: Lumbini, the Buddha's birthplace; Bodh Gaya, where he awakened; Sarnath, the site of his first teaching; and Kushinagar, the site of his death and parinirvana.

It was during a fourth Buddhist council, held by the Theravadins in Sri Lanka in the first century BCE, that the Buddha's oral teachings were finally written down, transcribed in Pali. The *Vinaya Pitaka*, the *Sutta Pitaka*—the collection of *suttas* (*sutras* in Sanskrit), discourses said to be delivered by the Buddha or his disciples—and the *Abhidhamma (Abhidharma* in Sanskrit*) Pitaka,* scholarly and philosophical analyses of the Buddha's main teachings, comprised the *Tipitaka (Tripitaka* in Sanskrit), "the three baskets." Known as the Pali Canon, the Tipitaka became the doctrinal basis of **Theravada**, the Teaching of the Elders. The tradition most closely associated with the Buddha's original teachings, Theravada spread across southern Asia.

Rise of Mahayana Buddhism

While Theravada continued to be the main thrust of Buddhism, during the first or early second century CE another tradition, Mahayana Buddhism, emerged. *Yana*, which means "vehicle" in both Pali and Sanskrit, refers to the method of practice by which one reaches enlightenment. Mahayana means the Great Vehicle, and the Mahayanists disparaged Theravada as Hinayana, the Lesser Vehicle. Mahayana doctrine embraced the same fundamental Buddhist teachings as Theravada, but it was sufficiently different to be called the Second Turning of the Wheel of Dharma.

The two traditions diverged on several points. While the focus of Theravada was the arahant, whose pursuit of enlightenment is single-minded, the Mahayana ideal was the bodhisattva, who seeks enlightenment not for personal gain but out of compassion, in order to help all beings awaken. The Theravadins aspired to acquire Buddha-like qualities, while Mahayanists believed that we are already Buddhas, already enlightened—we just don't know it. All beings have Buddha nature inherently, they said. We practice to awaken to it.

Though the historical Buddha remained at the center of Theravada doctrine, after his parinirvana, he was gone—only a fond memory to his followers. By contrast, the Mahayana Buddha was transcendent and ever present, dwelling in an otherworldly realm with Buddhas past and future and a pantheon of bodhisattvas, ready to be called on for help as needed.

For the Theravadins, the Pali Canon remained the doctrinal foundation. They took a dim view of the large body of scripture and commentaries the Mahayanists added, among them the Prajnaparamita Sutras, or Perfection of Wisdom texts, and the Lotus Sutra—all of which the Mahayanists claimed had been revealed directly by the Buddha.

As Buddhism moved to southeast Asia, it took root in Sri Lanka, Burma (now Myanmar), Thailand, Cambodia, Laos, Malaysia, and Indonesia. Today in those countries there are still saffron-robed monks walking with their begging bowls or tending the Buddhist temples that became the center of worship and a fixture of community life—a place for ordinary people to leave flowers and other offerings in the hope of securing a favorable rebirth.

Meanwhile, Mahayana Buddhism was making its way across northern Asia to China, Korea, Vietnam, Japan, and eventually Nepal, Tibet, and Mongolia. By the second century CE,

Theravada and Mahayana Buddhism had converged on China, most likely via the Silk Road, the vast network of trading routes that crisscrossed Asia. Confucianism was the dominant religion in China at the time, and the Chinese were wary of monastic Buddhism, concerned it might undermine loyalty to family and the Emperor. However, Pure Land Buddhism, a devotional Mahayana school that arrived from India in the fourth century CE, found a congenial home in China. Pure Land believers pray to Amitabha, the Buddha of Infinite Light, for rebirth in the Pure Land, Sukhavati. As Pure Land Buddhism spread to Japan, Korea, and Vietnam it became even more popular.

Chan/Zen

Though accounts differ, an Indian monk named Bodhidharma is generally credited with introducing **Chan** Buddhism to China in the fifth century CE; he became known as the first patriarch of Chan. *Chan* is Chinese for *dhyana*, the Sanskrit word for meditation. In one version of the story, Bodhidharma was staying near the Shaolin monastery on China's Mount Song and taught the monks his concentration practice. When he saw that their bodies were stiff from sitting long hours in meditation, he gave them exercises the monks later developed into kung fu.

There was a natural affinity between Chan and Taoism, a contemplative tradition that was China's other established religion, and Chan incorporated Taoist elements. Called **Zen** when it later arrived in Japan, Chan was a revelation—a Mahayana Buddhist school "unique in various ways in the history of religion," suggests Daisetz Teitaro Suzuki, a leading scholar of Mahayana Buddhism who played a key role in introducing

Zen to the West. In *An Introduction to Zen Buddhism,* he writes: "The deepest truths of Zen . . . cannot be made the subject of logical exposition. They are to be experienced in the inmost soul when they become for the first time intelligible." A "practical and systematic" method of mind training, Chan/Zen is "more than meditation . . . in its ordinary sense," Suzuki explains. "The discipline of Zen consists in opening the mental eye in order to look into the very nature of existence." Often referred to as "direct transmission outside the scripture," Chan/Zen is grounded in personal experience. Texts are considered "mere waste paper whose utility consists in wiping off the dirt of intellect and nothing more," Suzuki states. Despite that, a vast number of Chan and Zen texts exist, but the wise practitioner does not expect to awaken from reading a book. As a famous Zen saying warns, "A finger pointing at the moon is not the moon."

From China, Chan spread to Korea, where it is called Seon, and to Vietnam, where it is Thiền. In the mid-sixth century CE, monks from Korea introduced Buddhism to Japan. A number of Buddhist sects sprang up, none of them Zen. In 804 CE, Dengyo Daishi, a monk from China, arrived in Japan and established Tendai, which became the dominant Buddhist school in Japan from the ninth to the twelfth centuries CE.

Zen arrived in Japan in the twelfth century CE. Myoan Eisai, a Japanese Buddhist priest who had been studying Chan in China, returned to Japan and established the Rinzai Zen school. Along with Soto Zen, it remains one of the two main schools of Zen Buddhism in Japan. Eisai also introduced the tea ceremony, a ritual still closely associated with Zen practice. The samurai, Japan's military elite, readily embraced Rinzai Zen, a rigorous practice that relies on intense, one-pointed meditation called *zazen* and verbal conundrums called **koans** to awaken students. Based on the Linji school developed by a Chinese master known for his harsh teaching methods, Rinzai Zen was well suited to the disciplined warrior style of the samurai.

Koans are seemingly nonsensical, paradoxical questions unanswerable by reasoning that Zen masters assign their students to bring about awakening. Literally, koan means "public case"; it originally referred to a legal case that established a precedent. A koan might be a phrase from a teaching or a *mondo*—a collection of dialogues between teacher and student—or another source. The student works with the koan, on and off the cushion, for anywhere from minutes to years, until the conceptual mind gives up, and in a dramatic mental shift, the student "answers" the koan. The realization is like Zen **satori**, or sudden enlightenment that is a complete reorientation of ordinary mind to non-dualistic "original mind." Among the most quoted (and misquoted) koans are "What is the sound of one hand?" and "Show me your original face, the one before your mother and father were born." However, it is another koan, Joshu's Dog, that is likely to elicit a smile (or groan) of recognition from generations of Zen students who have mulled over the "case" as their entry koan. Case 1 in the thirteenth-century CE collection *Mumonkan* (the Gateless Barrier), it reads: *"A monk asked Joshu, 'Has a dog the Buddha nature?' Joshu answered, 'Mu'."*

In Zen, everyone is believed to have Buddha nature—"the nature of being inherently awake," as Robert Aitken Roshi (**Roshi** is Japanese for "old master") defined it in a Dharma talk about Case 1. So why the question—and why that answer? "To recognize one's own Buddha nature and the awakened nature of all things, even dogs, demands perception, direct seeing, direct intimacy," Aitken Roshi explained. "Mu, as a temporary skillful means, leads us to a moment, and to a life, where we exist in the world without commentary, without interpretation."

Koan practice is intense, and there's a famous line about that in the *Mumonkan*. Mumon Ekai (Wumen Huikai in Chinese), the compiler of the text, warns that practicing with Mu day and night "will be just as if you swallow a red-hot iron ball, which you cannot spit out even if you try." For those who stick with the practice, however, the reward is great. Although Mu translates as "no" or "nothingness," it "is not about negation," Roshi Joan Halifax emphasized in a talk at Upaya, her Zen center in Santa Fe, New Mexico. "It is about liberation: liberation from ideas, ideals, ideologies."

Soto Zen, the other major school of Japanese Zen practice and the more widely practiced today, is superficially less intense than Rinzai but, in its own way, no less demanding. The central practice is *shikantaza,* or "just sitting." There is no koan to solve, no focus of meditation, no goal but to be fully present and alert in every moment—on and off the cushion. Not as easy as it sounds.

As a young monk in Japan, Eihei Dogen Zenji, the founder of the Soto school, had a burning question: *Why, if everyone has Buddha nature, did Buddhas of the past seek enlightenment when they were already enlightened?* Armed with that and a desire to find authentic teachings, he went to China to study. His Chinese teacher soon died, but not before making Dogen his Dharma heir with permission to teach. Dogen returned to Japan and established Eihei-ji, one of the two head temples of the Soto school. Dogen is among the most revered of the Zen patriarchs, and almost every Zen student has encountered his teachings, not least the Genjo Koan, with its trenchant message: "To study Buddhism is to study the self. To study the self is to forget the self. To forget the self is to be enlightened by all things."

Soto practice sometimes includes koan study but not in the Rinzai manner. Dogen taught that daily life is a koan, explains Norman Fischer, founder of the Everyday Zen Foundation, which adapts Zen Buddhist teachings to Western culture. In "Who Hears This Sound," an introduction to koan study, Fischer writes:

> Dogen . . . devised a kind of koan practice that is particularly useful to contemporary practitioners, who might want to work with koans outside the context of regular retreats or daily temple life. In other words, people like us. He called this method Genjo Koan of the Present Moment . . . Dogen says, in effect, that the experience of being itself, moment after moment, is itself a koan . . . In the case of daily life practice, it might mean taking personal issues or themes that arise in one's life as koans for contemplation, rather than as objective issues that one is trying to work through for personal ease or advantage. I personally find the idea of Genjo Koan really useful as it affords us a way to view our lives as deep, spiritual journeys, rather than as mundane distractions to be transcended.

With Zen and Pure Land Buddhism already in place, another Buddhist school, Nichiren, appeared in Japan in the thirteenth century CE. Strictly homegrown, Nichiren, like Pure Land, is a devotional school, though its devotion is not to Amitabha Buddha but to the Lotus Sutra. Nichiren, who founded the school, believed that merely chanting *Namu myoho renge kyo* ("Homage to the Lotus of the Good Dharma Sutra") would lead to spiritual—and worldly—fulfillment. Adherents of a twentieth-century CE lay offshoot of Nichiren Buddhism, Soka Gakkai, repeat the same mantra with the aspiration for similar results. In recent years, Soka Gakkai has reportedly attracted an international following among celebrities, including singer Tina Turner, musician Herbie Hancock, and actors Orlando Bloom, Adewale Akinnuoye-Agbaje, and Miranda Kerr.

India

While Buddhism was fanning out across Asia, it was far from moribund in India. In the third century CE, the scholar Nagarjuna put forth the doctrine of Madhyamaka, or the Middle Way, one of the two most influential philosophical schools of Indian Mahayana Buddhism. Building on the Buddha's teachings on emptiness, Madhyamaka holds that phenomena do not exist independently but only in relation to one another and that the interrelatedness of all phenomena—dependent origination— is ultimate reality.

From the fifth to the twelfth century CE, the foremost center of Buddhist scholarship was Nalanda, a *mahavihara,* or large Buddhist monastery, in northern India in what is now Bihar state, bordering on Nepal. Nalanda's importance in the history of Buddhism cannot be overemphasized. Essential Mahayana teachings and much of Tibetan Buddhist doctrine can be traced in one way or another to the Nalanda masters.

Asanga and Vasubandhu, half-brothers who were Nalanda scholars in the fourth and fifth centuries CE, are credited with founding the second major school of Indian Mahayana Buddhism, Yogacara, although its key concepts were floated a century earlier, in texts like the Sandhinirmocana Sutra (Noble Sutra of the Explanation of the Profound Secrets). Dubbed the Mind-Only school, Yogacara (the name means "yoga practice") put forth several concepts that were particularly influential in Chan/Zen. Among the most important of these is the teaching on karma. Yogacara holds that there are eight consciousnesses, one of which is a "storehouse consciousness" that stores "karmic seeds" of which the mind is unaware until certain conditions arise, bringing the karma to fruition. This unconscious level of experience is where habits are formed and held. Our behavior creates these karmic patterns or "habit energies," which influence not only our own lives but also the lives of others.

The Surangama Sutra, an important text in Chan Buddhism that touts the supremacy of *samadhi*—deep concentration—as a vehicle for awakening, is also said to have originated at Nalanda. By the time Nalanda was destroyed by invaders in 1193 CE, Buddhism in northern India was already on the wane. The focus had shifted to Chan/Zen and Tibetan Buddhism.

Vajrayana

An outgrowth of Mahayana Buddhism, Vajrayana, the Diamond Vehicle, is viewed by some as the Third Turning of the Wheel of Dharma. Rooted in Indian *tantras*—esoteric teachings—it spread all across the Himalayan region and beyond. Known to most as Tibetan Buddhism, it is closely associated with Tibet, Nepal and Mongolia, as well as Ladakh, a Himalayan region in northern India nicknamed "Little Tibet," and Bhutan, where

Buddhism is the official state religion. Since 1959, when the Dalai Lama fled Tibet after the Chinese takeover, thousands of Tibetan refugees have resettled in India, other parts of Asia, and the West, bringing their Buddhist practices with them.

Buddhism reached Tibet, "the Land of the Snows," in the seventh century CE, where it encountered Bön, the shamanistic indigenous religion. Over the centuries, relations between Bön and Tibetan Buddhism were often uneasy, but they continued to influence each other to varying degrees. As practiced today, Bön contains many Buddhist elements.

In the seventh century CE, Tibet began opening up to the world. King Songtsen Gampo unified the country and expanded its borders, taking over Nepal, parts of northern India and northern Burma, and a chunk of China. This introduced him to Buddhism—and to his two Buddhist wives, from India and China, respectively. Songtsen Gampo built the first Buddhist temples in Tibet, including the Jokhang in the country's capital, Lhasa. Later he was recognized as an emanation of Avalokiteshvara, the bodhisattva of compassion, a tradition that has continued with Tibetan leaders ever since. In the eighth century CE, Buddhism became Tibet's state religion, and the king, Trisong Detsen, invited Chan masters from China and the Indian tantra masters Padmasambhava and Shantarakshita to visit.

The Nyingma

King Trisong Detsen asked Shantarakshita to build the first monastery in Tibet. When the local deities put up resistance, Shantarakshita suggested calling in Padmasambhava to appease them. Deities appeased, Padmasambhava finished the monastery, called Samye, and founded the Nyingma Order—"the Ancient Ones." The earliest of the four major schools of Tibetan Buddhism, Nyingma incorporated aspects of Bön, including *dzogchen* ("great perfection"), a powerful practice for directly experiencing the ground of being.

Padmasambhava is the most important figure in the establishment of Tibetan Buddhism, revered as Guru Rinpoche ("Precious Master") and after called "the second Buddha." His many miraculous feats are firmly entrenched in Tibetan lore, and he was said to have hidden **terma**, or "treasure texts"—important scriptures—for safekeeping, to be found later on by spiritual adepts called **tertons** ("revealers of sacred texts"). Some terma were physical—texts or ritual objects hidden in rocks or trees or submerged in lakes—while others were said to be housed in the mindstream of the tertons. Nyingma was largely a lay movement, with lay teachers, until the fourteenth century CE when it went on a monastery-building spree.

The period from the seventh to the ninth centuries CE is known as the first dissemination of Buddhism in Tibet. There was widespread acceptance of Buddhist teachings and ethics. Buddhism had a transformative effect on the Tibetans, according to Robert A. F. Thurman, a noted Buddhologist and professor of Indo-Tibetan Studies at Columbia University in New York. In *Wisdom and Compassion* he writes:

> *One must admire the achievement of Padmasambhava and Shan-*
> *tarakshita and their disciples, for it must have been difficult to*
> *persuade the rough warrior population of Tibet that nonviolence*
> *is the way to live, that self-conquest is more important than*
> *military conquest, that enlightened humanity is more important*

than national gods, and that the purpose of life is evolutionary
merit and transcendent wisdom, not power and pleasure.

The boom time for Buddhism ended with the assassination
of King Tri Ralpachen in 836. The new king persecuted Buddhist practitioners, destroyed temples and texts, and made Bön
the state religion.

After two centuries out of favor, the revival of Buddhism in
Tibet began in the eleventh century CE. The arrival in 1042
CE of the great Indian scholar Atisha signaled the beginning of
the second dissemination of Buddhism in Tibet. Buddhism was
restored as the state religion, and at the king's request, Atisha
wrote *Bodhipathapradipa*, A Lamp for the Path to Enlightenment,
an accessible guide to *lamrim*, the stages of the path to liberation.
Many versions of lamrim by different teachers have appeared
since, but all are based on Atisha's text.

The Sakya

The eleventh century CE also saw the establishment of the second major Tibetan Buddhist school, the Sakya Order, by the
Khön family, Tibetan nobility from the southern Tsang prov-
ince. Khön Könchok Gyalpo founded the Sakya monastery in
1073, and male members of the Khön family have headed the
Sakyas in one unbroken line ever since. Under a new method
of succession, the head of the order, the Sakya Trizin ("Sakya
Throneholder"), now serves a three-year term, instead of for
life. The current head of the lineage is the 42nd Sakya Trizen,
Ratna Vajra Rinpoche, installed in March 2017.

After the Mongols took over Tibet in the thirteenth century, the Sakyas were recruited to teach Buddhism to the Mongol leaders. Sakya lamas became the court priests and were appointed to various government posts until by the 1350s, Tibet was under Sakya control. The Sakyapa (*pa* means "followers") are known for their scholarship. Their central teaching is the Lamdré, meditation instruction on the spiritual path and its fruit that is based on the Hevajra Tantra (Wisdom-Mother Tantra). In Tibetan iconography, Hevajra—a *yidam*, or enlightened being—is depicted in union with his consort, Nairatmya, a female Buddha whose name means "she who has no ego."

The Kagyu

As the Sakya Order was starting up in the eleventh century CE, a Tibetan layman named Marpa was emerging as a Tibetan Buddhist force. In his travels to India, Marpa received profound teachings from great masters, including the adept Naropa. Marpa's translations of Buddhist texts from Sanskrit into Tibetan earned him the sobriquet Marpa the Translator.

With hundreds of disciples, Marpa formed the Kagyu ("Oral Tradition") Order, the third major school of Tibetan Buddhism. The name came not from Marpa's countless translations but from his teacher Naropa's "precious" instructions on tantra practices. Of Marpa's four most important disciples, the most famous was Milarepa, a celebrated singer and poet who often delivered teachings in the form of Tibetan folk songs. It was Milarepa's personal transformation, however, that was most inspiring—a tale of spiritual redemption and the power of Buddhist practice.

Milarepa's birth name, Mila Thopaga, means "joy to hear,"

but after his father died and his aunt and uncle absconded with the family's money, Mila's mother made him learn sorcery to support the family. Mila spent years wreaking havoc with his black magic until one day his evil ways went sour, and he turned to Marpa for Buddhist instruction. Marpa, however, sent him away. Mila then lied to get another teacher to take him on, but when he confessed to the teacher that Marpa had rejected him, he was told he would never make spiritual progress until he squared things with Marpa. Put through a grueling initiation, Mila was finally accepted by Marpa as a student. After years of practice as a wandering monk, Mila achieved enlightenment and received a new name: Milarepa, "Cotton-Clad Great One."

Like his teacher, Milarepa had hundreds of disciples. He placed one of them, Gampopa, also known as Dakpo Lhaje, in charge of developing the Kagyu order. Gampopa's enlightened disciples in turn formed branches of the order. (There are now many suborders too.) One of Gampopa's disciples, Dusum Khyenpa, the first Karmapa—an honorific meaning "Victorious One"—established the *tulku* system, a practice unique to Tibetan Buddhism that consists of formally recognizing reincarnations of great lamas to continue their lineages. Before his death, Dusum Khyenpa left word where he would be reborn, a custom that continues to be practiced by tulkus. (Dusum Khyenpa was reborn as Karma Pakshi, the teacher of Kublai Khan, the thirteenth-century CE Mongol emperor.)

The Kagyus also are known for *Mahamudra* (Great Seal), advanced practices on the pristine nature of mind. ("Seal" is a reference to the stamp used to authenticate documents, or in this case, the essential doctrine.)

As the head of the Kagyu lineage, the Karmapa is third in the

Tibetan Buddhist hierarchy behind the Dalai Lama and the Sakya Trizin. In recent years, the Karma Kagyus—one of the four main branches of the Kagyu Order and the most widely practiced—have been embroiled in controversy over who is currently the rightful seventeeth Karmapa, with each of two rival factions claiming that their candidate is the one. Ogyen Trinley Dorje has been confirmed as the rightful one by the Dalai Lama and a majority of the Kagyu high lamas. Born in Tibet in 1985, he escaped to India in 2000, and since then has lived in Dharamsala under virtual house arrest, while nominally a guest of the Indian government. The other contender—Trinley Thaye Dorje, born in 1983—escaped Tibet in 1994 and was recognized as the Karmapa by the fourteenth Shamar Rinpoche, the second most senior lama in the Karma Kagyu order. Now living in New Delhi, Thaye Dorje left the monkhood in 2017 to marry—an unusual move for Karmapas. He still claims the Karmapa title but no longer ordains monastics. In a groundbreaking meeting in southern France in 2018, the two Karmapas discussed how to heal the rift in the Karma Kagyu order.

The Kadam

In the mid-eleventh century CE, the Kadam Order was founded by Dromtön, a lay master who was a disciple of Atisha. He based the order on Atisha's teachings. The Kadampa were known for their serious practice and teachings on *bodhicitta*, the compassionate aspiration to awaken for the benefit of all beings. Unlike the Sakya and Kagyu orders, the Kadam steered clear of involvement in Tibet's political affairs. Eventually, the Kadam teachings were folded into the Gelug Order, also known as the New Kadam Order.

The Gelug

The Gelug Order is the youngest of the four major schools of Tibetan Buddhism. It was founded in the fourteenth century CE by the monk Je Tsongkhapa, who had studied under Nyingma, Sakya, and Kagyu teachers all over Tibet.

Tsongkhapa put together a number of teachings from the different schools. He took the Kadam teachings on *lojong* (mind training) and *lamrim* (stages of the path) and combined them with Sakya tantra teachings, then stirred in traditional Buddhist teachings on the Vinaya and ethics, added Dharma debate, and came up with a comprehensive course of study. The Gelugpa emphasized monastic discipline, and Tsongkhapa founded multiple monasteries, including Ganden, Drepung, Sera, and the Potala in Lhasa. A reformer who sought to revive monastic discipline, Tsongkhapa had his monks wear yellow hats, to distinguish them from monks in the Nyingma, Sakya, and Kagyu traditions, who wore the red hats favored by the *pandits,* the learned masters at Nalanda monastery. Thus, the Gelugpa became known as the Yellow Hat Order.

After Tsongkhapa died in 1419, the Gelugpa began feverishly building monasteries all over Tibet and even one in Beijing. When Tsongkhapa's successor Gendun Drubpa died, a child was identified as his reincarnation, and the tulku system developed by the Kagyus kicked into action. A few reincarnations later, Sonam Gyatso, born in 1543, was invited to visit the Mongol chief and ended up converting the Mongols en masse. The head of the Mongols was so grateful he proclaimed Sonam the third Dalai Lama. (The previous two incarnations were appointed retroactively.)

Dalai is Mongolian for "ocean" or "big," and *lama* is Tibetan for "master" or "guru." Every Dalai Lama is believed to be the incarnation of Avalokiteshvara, the bodhisattva of compassion, known as Chenrezig in Tibetan. The fifth Dalai Lama, born in 1617, was the first to be declared political as well as spiritual leader of Tibet, a role the Dalai Lamas filled until 2011. While the Dalai Lama remains the spiritual leader, Tibet's government-in-exile is now headed by a secular, elected prime minister.

Second to the Dalai Lama in the Gelug tradition is the Panchen Lama. Just as today there is a controversy over the seventeenth Karmapa, the legitimacy of the eleventh Panchen Lama has been under debate. After the death of the tenth Panchen Lama in 1989, a dispute arose between the Chinese government and His Holiness Tenzin Gyatso, the fourteenth Dalai Lama, over his successor. In 1995, His Holiness recognized a six-year-old, Gedhun Choekyi Nyima, as the eleventh Panchen Lama. The Chinese, apparently miffed that the Dalai Lama had named a Panchen Lama without their approval, seized the boy and his family, and claimed legitimacy for a candidate of their own, Gyaincain Norbu. As of 2017 the Dalai Lama's candidate was still being held in a secret location by the Chinese, who had also imprisoned the head of the search committee. Then in 2018, the Dalai Lama received "reliable word" that Gedhun Choekyi Nyima was alive and receiving a "normal" education. In a surprise reversal, His Holiness acknowledged that there could be two legitimate reincarnations of the Panchen Lama, although only one could hold the official seat. Supporters of the Chinese candidate took that to mean His Holiness was acknowledging theirs as the "official" Panchen Lama. The Panchen Lama controversy has been linked to an even greater concern: indications that when the Dalai Lama dies, the Chinese are intent on naming his successor.

The intrusion of the Chinese into Tibetan affairs, including those of a spiritual nature, has been dispiriting to the Dalai Lama and the Tibetan people. Hundreds of monasteries in Tibet were destroyed during the Cultural Revolution, and only a few have been allowed to rebuild. The vitality, indeed the continued existence, of Tibetan Buddhism and Tibetan culture going forward may well rest on Tibetans in exile and Westerners who have taken up Tibetan Buddhist practice and the Tibetan cause.

Coming to the West

Tibetan Buddhism had existed more or less without incident until 1951, when the Chinese effectively took control of Tibet, and there was brutal repression of the Tibetan people. Finally, following the Tibetan uprising in 1959, His Holiness Tenzin Gyatso, the fourteenth Dalai Lama, was forced to flee. He made a harrowing escape over the Himalayas to India, where he established the Tibetan community and Tibetan government in exile in Dharamsala.

As the Chinese systematically destroyed monasteries in Tibet and killed or imprisoned Tibetan Buddhist monastics, others who managed to flee joined the wave of Tibetans arriving in India. Jawaharlal Nehru, India's Prime Minister at the time, asked an Englishwoman, Freda Bedi, to help settle the refugees.

Bedi, who later become the first Westerner ordained as a Tibetan Buddhist nun, started a school for the young lamas and tulkus whose monastic education had been interrupted by the Tibetan diaspora. A high priority was learning English so they could eventually teach Tibetan Buddhism to Westerners. Bedi's star pupils were two tulkus, Chögyam Trungpa and Chöjë Akong, who later established Samye Ling in Scotland, the first Tibetan Buddhist monastery in the West. While Akong Rinpoche remained in Europe, Trungpa Rinpoche came to the United States to teach.

Buddhism in America

Ever since the Pilgrims cast off from Plymouth, England, people from all over the world have been coming to America to make a fresh start. It was that way with Buddhism too. The Zen masters who began arriving at the beginning of the twentieth century CE could no more be sure what they would find or what their reception would be than could those first Europeans who set out for the New World. Once the Zen masters arrived, with no structure to support Buddhism in America they relaxed their strict monastic training in their approach to the free-and-easy Westerners. Amazingly, the Dharma took.

The Zen transplants took care to preserve the teachings, but they adapted with remarkable agility to a new language, unfamiliar lifestyle, and students who were simultaneously naive and demanding—in sometimes puzzling ways. Americans, for their part, were fascinated by the Asian teachers and the exoticism of the teachings and practices they brought with them.

When Buddhism entered America, it landed first on the East and West coasts, with a touchdown in Chicago. It was at the Columbian Exposition in Chicago in 1893 that America got its first glimpse of a Buddhist monk. Among those attending the World Parliament of Religions at the exposition were a Sri Lankan Buddhist monk, Anagarika Dharmapala, and a Rinzai Zen master, Soyen Shaku. Soyen Shaku returned a few years later to teach a family of wealthy Californians living near San Francisco. Not long after that, his student, Nyogen Senzaki, who was serving as the family's houseboy, began what he called "rolling zendos"—teaching small groups mostly in people's living rooms.

One by one, the number of Zen practitioners in America grew. Unlike Asian immigrants, who brought their religion with them, these "convert" Buddhists had been raised in some other tradition—mostly Christian or Jewish. (D. T. Suzuki, who was fluent in the English language and Western religions, often served as a go-between.) Many of the early converts in America were wealthy and well-traveled, and could afford to support the visiting teachers and provide the funds to rent or buy or build places for them to teach and live.

Among those supporters was Ruth Fuller Everett, who had briefly studied with D. T. Suzuki and Nanshinken Roshi in Japan. In 1932, she became the principal benefactor of Sokei-an Shigetsu Sasaki and the Buddhist Society of America he had founded two years earlier in New York City. Sokei-an had first arrived in America in 1906 with his teacher, Sokatsu Shaku, to set up a lay Zen community in California. When the community folded in 1910, Sokei-an stayed on, working at odd jobs—

farm hand, art restorer, humorist, and janitor among them—while returning periodically to Japan to ordain as a Zen priest, before finally settling in New York.

Not surprisingly, World War II cut off the flow of Zen teachers from Japan. Those who were already here were marked as resident aliens and interned. Sokei-an, severely weakened by his stay in the camps, won early release in 1943. He married Ruth Everett, by then a widow, but his health deteriorated further and he died within a year. Ruth Sasaki returned to Japan as the head temple priest at a Rinzai Zen monastery in Kyoto, and continued to be influential in establishing Zen in America until her death in 1967.

By the 1950s, Zen was making inroads on the West Coast. Allen Ginsberg introduced the Beat poets in San Francisco to Zen, and soon Jack Kerouac, Neal Cassady, Gary Snyder, Philip Whalen, and others were meditating and weaving Buddhist imagery into their writing. Ruth Sasaki's son-in-law, Alan Watts, a philosopher and writer newly arrived from England, was influential in introducing Buddhist ideas in language Westerners understood.

In the 1950s, a few intrepid Westerners, following Ruth Sasaki's lead, went to Japan to study in Zen monasteries and then brought home what they had learned. Robert Aitken Roshi opened a Zen center in Hawaii, and Philip Kapleau Roshi founded the Rochester Zen Center in upstate New York. Kapleau's book *The Three Pillars of Zen* described in detail the *satori*—sudden enlightenment—experiences of Japanese and Western practitioners, convincing skeptical Americas that Buddhist meditation could indeed lead to awakening.

The year 1959 was a turning point in the history of Buddhism in America. Shunryu Suzuki Roshi, a Soto Zen priest, visited from Japan and was so impressed he decided to stay on. He had become disillusioned with Japanese Zen, where the temple priests performed weddings and funerals but had little interest in meditation. Americans were more open and receptive to Buddhist practice, Suzuki Roshi found. He, in turn, was astute at conveying the Dharma to a sangha consisting largely of young people, hipsters, and intellectuals. His bestselling book *Zen Mind, Beginner's Mind* introduced Zen practice to a whole generation of spiritual seekers. Very soon the San Francisco Zen Center became the nexus of Buddhist practice on the West Coast, expanding its reach when it built Tassajara, the first Soto Zen monastery in America, in the mountains behind Big Sur. (Later, after Suzuki Roshi's death, SFZC opened another practice center, Green Gulch Farm, in Marin County.) The 1960s brought the arrival of more Zen masters, including the influential teachers Taizan Maezumi Roshi and Joshu Sasaki Roshi, who established sanghas in California. By decade's end, the West Coast Buddhist scene was thriving with a mystique all its own.

Back East, Zen was also expanding, but in slightly less exuberant fashion. In 1956, Ruth Fuller Sasaki renamed the Buddhist Society of America as the First Zen Institute. That same year, the Zen Studies Society opened Shobo-ji, a Rinzai Zen center in New York City founded to help D. T. Suzuki disseminate Zen in the West. It was organized around the teachings of the Japanese masters Soen Nakagawa Roshi and Nyogen Senzaki. Tai Shimano, later ordained as Eido Shimano Roshi, was installed as resident teacher. In 1976, Eido Roshi presided over the opening of Dai Bosatsu Zendo Kongo-ji, the first Rinzai Zen monastery in the West. Overlooking a mist-shrouded lake in New York State's Catskill Mountains, it was modeled on Japan's largest Rinzai monastery, Tofukuji, in Kyoto.

By then, Zen wasn't the only Buddhist show in town. In 1970, Chögyam Trungpa Rinpoche, the Tibetan Buddhist lama who had been schooled in Western ways by Freda Bedi in India, began teaching in the United States. Over the next decade, he established practice centers he called *dharmadhatus*—Sanskrit for "Dharma realms"—in cities all over the US, and in Boulder, Colorado, he founded Naropa Institute, later Naropa University. The first college in America devoted exclusively to Buddhist studies, Naropa drew teachers and practitioners in the three main Buddhist traditions to its popular summer programs.

Trungpa Rinpoche was an unorthodox, often outrageous but brilliant teacher who was the face of Tibetan Buddhism in America until he died of a heart attack in 1983 at the age of forty-eight. Despite Trungpa Rinpoche's popularity, however, Tibetan Buddhism was slower to catch on in America than Zen. In part, that was because Tibetan Buddhist monks, like the Zen masters before them, had to become sufficiently fluent in English and grounded in the culture to connect with Western students. But the biggest factor was the nature of Tibetan Buddhist practice in itself.

Tibetan Buddhism is largely guru-centered. The visualizations, empowerments, and secret teachings rely on the teacher to guide the student through what may be many years of practice. To newcomers, the rituals and initiations can seem bewilderingly arcane. But after the Dalai Lama's first visit to the US in 1979, interest in Tibetan Buddhism picked up. More lamas arrived, many of whom had been raised in India, were fluent in English, and could more readily adapt to American ways.

A handful of Tibetan Buddhist teachers had already quietly settled in America. On the West Coast, Tarthang Tulku founded the first Nyingma meditation center in the US, in Berkeley, California, in 1969. More than a decade earlier, in 1958, Geshe Ngawang Wangyal, a Kalmyk-Mongolian lama, opened the first Tibetan Buddhist monastery in the US, in Freehold, New Jersey. (Geshe, "virtuous friend" in Tibetan, is a Tibetan Buddhist academic degree roughly equivalent to a Ph.D.) Geshe Wangyal's student Robert Thurman became the first American to take vows as a Tibetan Buddhist monk in Asia.

Tibetan Buddhist monastic training is rigorous, but other Americans began to follow Thurman to Asia. Some, like Lama Surya Das, born Jeffrey Miller, returned to the US to teach meditation. Others landed in academia, including Thurman, who was named to the first endowed chair in Buddhist Studies in the West, the Jey Tsong Khapa Chair in Indo-Tibetan Buddhist Studies at Columbia University. A charismatic teacher in and out of the classroom and a popular author, Thurman has been instrumental in introducing Tibetan Buddhism to the general public. A longtime friend of the Dalai Lama, Thurman, along with actor Richard Gere and composer Philip Glass, founded Tibet House in 1987 to support Tibetan culture among Tibetans who have resettled outside Tibet.

In the early 1970s, Jack Kornfield and Joseph Goldstein, two ex–Peace Corps workers who had trained in **Vipassana** (Insight meditation) in Asia, returned to the US and, after attending the summer program at Naropa, decided to teach. In

1976, joined by Sharon Salzberg, another American who had studied Vipassana in Asia, the three founded the Insight Meditation Society in Barre, Massachusetts. IMS was the first center in America to teach Vipassana and quickly became popular for making the practices of renowned Asian meditation masters like U Pandita, Mahasi Sayadaw U Sobhana, Anagarika Munindra, Ajahn Chah, and S. N. Goenka user-friendly for Americans. Guest teachers, including some of the Asian masters, joined the founders in teaching Vipassana meditation in ten-day retreats and three-month training periods. Kornfield later moved to California and in 1988, with some other teachers, opened Spirit Rock, an Insight meditation center in the woodlands of West Marin County that became the hub of Vipassana practice on the West Coast.

Maintaining silence 24/7 for a week, never mind three months, was practically unheard of outside Catholic monasteries in America at the time. But as more Buddhist teachers cropped up around the country—many of them American students of the Asian Zen masters or the IMS founders—more opportunities for practice opened up, and suddenly meditation was hip. In 1979, Jon Kabat-Zinn, a longtime meditator who was founder and executive director of the Center for Mindfulness in Medicine, Health Care, and Society at the University of Massachusetts Medical School and its Stress Reduction Clinic, launched Mindfulness-Based Stress Reduction, an eight-week program grounded in Buddhist meditation techniques that became an instant hit with the health-care community and took meditation mainstream. Backed by clinical studies, MBSR helped launch the mindfulness movement that has swept the country.

The 1970s and 1980s spawned a golden era in American Buddhism, as all three Buddhist traditions put down roots in the US. For scores of practitioners—mostly young, educated, and white—Buddhist practice offered a spiritual counterweight to the self-involvement of the Me Decade. In 1983, Chögyam Trungpa established a Tibetan Buddhist monastery, Gampo Abbey, in Nova Scotia, with Pema Chödrön, an American-born nun, as its abbot. Since then, as awareness of Tibetan Buddhism has grown, Tibetan lamas have continued to arrive in America, and Vajrayana centers have opened across the continent.

The burgeoning of Buddhism in the West has had another effect: reinvigorating Buddhist practice in the East. The flow of Western Dharma students to Asia has continued. And in 2012, Rato Khen Rinpoche—Geshe Thupten Lhundup, a Gelug monk born Nicholas Vreeland and raised in the West—was appointed abbot of Rato Dratsang (*Dratsang* means "school" or "university" in Tibetan) in the Indian state of Karnataka. Dratsang, which is under the patronage of the Dalai Lama, was an important monastery in Tibet for centuries. Geshe Vreeland is the first Westerner to head a Tibetan Buddhist monastery in Asia. He also remains director of Kunkhyab Thardo Ling— The Tibet Center—in New York City.

A New Vehicle Emerging?

Today, as a second and even third generation of Western-born Buddhist teachers put their stamp on the Dharma, the landscape of Buddhism in America is changing fast. Women—

marginalized in traditional Buddhist practice despite the Buddha's initial efforts—are assuming a more prominent role, and the demand for multiculturalism and gender diversity is beginning to reshape sanghas. American Buddhism's unacknowledged biases have never squared with the Buddha's teachings on equality and the interconnection of all beings, and increasingly, teachers and Dharma centers are wrestling with ways to remedy inequities and reach out to all.

It is not just the face of American Buddhism that has changed in recent years. As teachers and sanghas undergo transformation, new forms for delivering the Dharma are cropping up. The internet and social media have created cyber-sanghas, with teachers transmitting the Dharma through podcasts and even leading retreats in real time via video conferencing technology like Skype and Zoom. No longer is the local meditation center necessarily the hub of practice. And apps for the cell phone have put every kind of practice at one's fingertips—literally— complete with guided meditations and digital gongs to signal the beginning and end of a practice period.

As delivery methods are changing, so too are the teachings themselves, which are evolving or being eliminated altogether with the changing times. Buddhism's nonsectarian approach appeals to youthful iconoclasts accustomed to bending traditional forms to accommodate contemporary goals. Secular Buddhist communities like Dharma Punx offer big-tent inclusiveness. And there is a growing movement of groups marrying the twelve-step recovery model and Buddhist practice, to address the mounting problem of addiction in America.

Perhaps the biggest change as Buddhism is transplanted in the West is in Theravada Buddhism, Dharma teacher Gil

Fronsdal has suggested. A former Soto Zen priest who was a Theravada monk in Burma and now teaches Vipassana in California, Fronsdal is not unusual among Western Buddhists in having studied and practiced in more than one Buddhist tradition. Many of today's practitioners hold the view that syncretism, if approached consciously, can enrich Buddhist practice rather than dilute or distort it, as traditionalists fear.

The Insight Meditation movement, according to Fronsdal, "is not simply a transplant of an Asian Buddhist tradition" but a new tradition altogether. Organized around Vipassana, or Insight meditation, the movement has dispensed with the rituals and monasticism of traditional Theravada, and some teachers have even done away with core tenets like rebirth and making merit. At the same time, practice has broadened from focusing on individual awakening to cultivating interpersonal qualities like generosity and kindness that have far-reaching collective benefits.

Is the Mahayana bodhisattva ideal of altruism and awakening to benefit others (see page 105) reshaping Theravada to fit Western values around compassionate service, human rights, and social justice? **Engaged Buddhism**, which applies the insights of Buddhist teachings and practices to social, political, and environmental concerns, has been steadily gaining traction. The term *Engaged Buddhism* was coined by the Vietnamese Zen monk Thich Nhat Hanh, who was exiled from his country for his efforts to promote peace and relieve suffering during the Vietnam War. Undaunted, Thây, as he is known to followers, moved to France in 1966 and established the Order of Interbeing—monastics and lay practitioners committed to living according to bodhisattva teachings on the interdependence of all beings. Since then, his books have introduced millions to cultivating

mindfulness and a peaceful heart, and he travels the world teaching Buddhism as a way of life and a vehicle for social change.
Thich Nhat Hanh's Fourteen Precepts of Engaged Buddhism
offer positive guidance for daily life in terms that are meaningful today. Along with traditional injunctions like "Do not kill"
are practical reminders like "Do not mistreat your body. Learn
to handle it with respect" and compassionate pleas like "Do not
accumulate wealth while millions are hungry."

Engaged Buddhists today are involved in projects ranging
from hospice care and conscious dying to prison Dharma, peace
initiatives, gender issues, environmental preservation, and animal
rights. Longtime advocates like Joanna Macy, Sulak Sivaraksa,
Taigen Dan Leighton, and Roshi Joan Halifax, and organizations
like the Buddhist Peace Fellowship and Buddhist Global Relief
are being joined by ad hoc internet and social media projects
through which young Buddhists are working to relieve suffering in all forms. The understanding behind all these effort is
that suffering affects not just individuals but also families,
communities, society at large, and the natural world. Politicians,
business leaders, media providers, and other influencers are
bringing mindfulness and compassion to their decision-making.
Through organizations like the Center for Contemplative Mind
in Society, started by Mirabai Bush in 1997, lawyers, manage-
ment consultants, educators, and the military have learned how
mindful presence can improve their efficiency, communications,
and humanity. During the Obama administration, Buddhist
leaders met in Washington, DC, to discuss how Buddhists
could play a more active role in civic life, around issues like cli-
mate change, education, and disarmament.

Engaged Buddhism is grounded in traditional teachings on

compassion, non-harming, and interconnection, but linking Buddhist principles and practices to community action and social justice is a contemporary, largely Western, concern. There are critics who argue that social activists are misappropriating the Dharma and perverting the Buddha's original intent—to guide practitioners to enlightenment—but for the most part Engaged Buddhism has found widespread support as a practical and timely way to address critical problems in today's world.

Dharma-inflected social action is once again demonstrating how flexible as well as resilient Buddhism is. As Western Buddhists successfully nudge the ancient teachings in new directions, more possibilities are opening up. The Pluralism Project, a Harvard University initiative on religious diversity, calls Engaged Buddhism "a major component of a growing American Buddhist ecumenical movement."

Where Buddhism will go next is for a new generation to decide. The issues facing the world today challenge everyone to think creatively and come up with practical, humane, and timely solutions. Buddhist practice at its most basic trains us to slow down, think clearly, stay in the present, let go of self-centered fear, and keep an open mind and heart. And above all, not to run away from whatever presents itself. Every human being has Buddha nature—natural goodness—the teachings say. We just need to learn to access it. And when it seems that problems are intractable and solutions hopeless, we can sit with that great truth the Buddha taught us: impermanence. Like it or not, everything changes.

It's tempting to speculate on what the Buddha would think about the multiple Buddhisms that have appeared over the past two millennia and the new ones emerging today. What would he say about the ways in which Buddhadharma has been stretched like taffy to accommodate changing mores in a fragmented and fractious world? What might he say about the Secular Buddhist movement, which looks to the Buddha's basic teachings before centuries of accretions obscured the simplicity of the message: that there is suffering in life and a way to the end of suffering? We can awaken to true happiness.

The Buddha told us we should not accept his—or anyone's—teachings as true without investigating them for ourselves, and only when we know them to be wise and beneficial, leading to happiness, should we adopt them. An overview of the teachings is the subject of the next chapter.

3

THE TEACHINGS

The Buddha did not refer to his teachings as Buddhism, any more than Jesus described his as Christianity. It remained for later commentators to affix the label *Buddhism* to what the Buddha merely referred to as the Dharma.

Wrapping one's arms around the Buddha's teachings is, in one sense, a challenge. The *Tipitaka*—the collection of Pali-language texts that form the basis of Theravada Buddhism, the Doctrine of the Elders—contains more than ten thousand discourses delivered by the Buddha or his disciplines during his forty-five-year teaching career. And that isn't even *all* the teachings, just the ones that have survived.

In the forest one day, the Buddha leaned down, scooped up a handful of leaves, and asked, "What do you think, monks? Which are more numerous, the few Simpasa leaves in my hand or those overhead in the forest?" Naturally the monks said those in the forest. "In the same way," the Buddha told them, "those things I have known with direct knowledge but have not taught are far more numerous (than what I have taught)." The reason he didn't pass on everything he knew, he said, was that he taught only what would lead to enlightenment and the end of suffering.

As noted in chapter 2, the Buddha's teachings were not transcribed until some three hundred years after his parinirvana. His monks listened carefully to the sermons and repeated them to one another, some amassing prodigious stores of memorized material in the process. Today Buddhist practitioners have written texts to rely on, but many teachers recommend listening to teachings rather than reading them. Not only does it require close attention but it creates a connection between teacher and student. Direct transmission of the Dharma from teacher to student is central to Zen and Tibetan Buddhist practice. Happily, teachings in all Buddhist traditions are widely available online (see Resources).

Like many oral traditions, early Buddhism relied on repetition and mnemonics to help keep the dharma straight. There are literally hundreds of numbered lists used as memory aids, among them: Three Marks of Existence, Three Poisons (mental defilements), Three Refuges, Three Types of Suffering, Four Noble Truths, Four Stages of Enlightenment, Four Foundations of Mindfulness, Five Aggregates, Five Hindrances, Five Precepts, Six Senses, Seven Factors of Enlightenment, Eight Worldly Concerns, Eightfold Path, Ten Perfections, Ten Fetters, Twelve Links of Dependent Origination, and Thirty-seven Factors of Enlightenment.

For a religion or philosophy with no supreme deity, no Bible, no church, no central authority, and, if the Buddha had his way, no leader, Buddhism is as complex a body of teachings and practices as you are likely to find. Much of that is because there is no one Buddhist doctrine. Since the Buddha's time, different schools have emerged, each with its own set of teachings and texts. Certain core teachings run through all three traditions—Theravada, Mahayana, and Vajrayana—and that's what this chapter focuses on, along with teachings specific to each tradition. But over the past two thousand years, a dizzying array of texts and commentaries interpreting the teachings have emerged. And today there is an entire literature of teachings by contemporary Buddhist teachers in every tradition.

The Buddha's teaching method was unorthodox for his time. He taught by skillful means—or, as it is sometimes called, skill in means. Whether he was addressing a crowd of ten thousand or an audience of one, he tailored his teaching to his listeners' level of experience and what he intuited they could grasp. Not all of what the Buddha taught was original with him: he was well schooled in the Hindu and Jain doctrine and practices of his, and was not afraid to draw on them when they would lead toward awakening. But experientially, he was unsurpassed, having investigated the mind so deeply and reached a level of spiritual attainment beyond that of others at the time. The Buddha wasn't into intellectual game playing and refused to engage in philosophical speculation. His teachings were practical, not doctrinal. He was concerned above all with what would lead to enlightenment—to the freedom and true happiness of the awakened mind. The frills and ruffles in the Dharma came along with later teachers and thinkers.

Physician of the Mind

The Buddha is often described as a physician who diagnosed the essential "disease" of life—suffering—then identified the causes and showed the way to a cure. The nontheistic, empirical foundation of Buddhism has made it popular with people of all faiths and no faith. The teachings have attracted atheists, agnostics, and seekers from other traditions, including, in the Buddha's day, many Brahmin priests. In recent decades, Buddhism and neuroscience have engaged in a fruitful dialogue, and there is a growing body of research on contemplative science and the mind, much of it with Buddhists participating as researchers and subjects. Tenzin Gyatso, the fourteenth Dalai Lama, has inspired much of this investigation. His Holiness has said that if the findings of science were to prove Buddhist teachings wrong, Buddhism would have to change. So far that hasn't happened. The Dharma has proved resilient.

THE FIRST TURNING OF THE WHEEL OF THE DHARMA

The Mahayana Buddhists came up with the device of the Three Turnings of the Wheel of Dharma as a way of sorting the original Pali suttas from the Sanskrit Mahayana sutras.

The wheel is an ancient spiritual symbol, an auspicious sign predating the Buddha. The wheel of Dharma, or *dhammacakka* (*dharmackra* in Sanskrit), was adopted by the Buddha's followers as the symbol of his teachings. The eight spokes represent the Noble Eightfold Path, the Buddha's action plan for awakening. The rim represents practice, which holds the teachings together. The hub stands for discipline.

The First Turning of the Wheel of Dharma refers to the teachings of the historical Buddha and his senior monks as set out in the Pali Canon. The text with the jaw-breaking name—

Dhammacakkappavattana Sutta—records the Buddha's first teaching, at the Deer Park in Sarnath, near Varanasi, when he explained the Four Noble Truths and the Middle Way to the five ascetics.

The teachings in the First Turning were geared toward the Buddha's early followers to help them attain individual liberation. They include not only the Four Noble Truths, the Eightfold Path, and the Middle Way but also other foundational teachings of the Pali Canon that are recognized by all three Buddhist traditions, such as karma, dependent origination, samsara and nirvana, *anatta* (non-self), *anicca* (impermanence), rebirth, and the Five Aggregates.

The Four Noble Truths

The First Turning of the Wheel of Dharma introduced the Four Noble Truths. They are said to contain the whole of the teachings:

> *The first noble truth:* There is suffering.
> *The second noble truth:* There is a cause of suffering.
> *The third noble truth:* There is an end to suffering.
> *The fourth noble truth:* There is a way of practice to end suffering.

Why call these truths *noble*? They're noble, the Buddha said, because it was his perfect comprehension of these truths that made him a Buddha, a Noble One. Bhadantacariya Buddhaghosa, the fifth century CE author of a famous commentary, the *Visuddhimagga* (The Path of Purification), suggested that the truths embody the qualities to be developed by anyone aspiring to become a noble one, like the Buddha.

Stephen Batchelor, a Buddhist teacher, scholar, and former monk in both the Zen and Tibetan Buddhist traditions, supports going back to the fundamental teachings of the Buddha and seeing the Four Noble Truths not as *truths*—absolute statements about reality—to be believed but as *actions* to perform. Elsewhere in the Pali Canon, he says, the word *sacca* refers "to the virtue of being truthful, honest, loyal, and sincere. Truth is seen as an ethical practice rather than a metaphysical claim." The Four Truths, then, are calls to action.

Whether you think of them as action steps or beliefs, the Four Noble Truths are intended to point whoever hears them toward awakening. Ajahn Sumedho, a teacher in the Thai forest tradition, thinks of them as *insights*—wisdom the Buddha discovered that we can now realize for ourselves.

THE FIRST NOBLE TRUTH: There is suffering.

The Pali word *dukkha*, usually translated as "suffering," equally means dissatisfaction, stress, distress, misery, agony, sorrow, anxiety, or, as Stephen Batchelor puts it, anguish. Dukkha is one of the Three Marks of Existence, or characteristics of samsara, conditioned reality. "Birth is suffering, aging is suffering, death is suffering," the Buddha said. "Sorrow, grief, pain, distress, and despair are suffering; separation from what is loved is suffering; not getting what is wanted is suffering."

We might wonder what is *not* covered by that definition. The Buddha identified three levels of suffering. The first is the suffering of suffering (*dukkha-dukkha*), predictable stresses of life like old age, sickness, and death; physical pain; not getting what we want; losing what we have; being in unpleasant situations; dealing with difficult people. This is ordinary suffering. It's not pleasant but it's unavoidable, so we develop strategies to deal with it.

The next level of suffering the Buddha identified as the suffering of change (*viparinama-dukkha*). Even the people, places, experiences, and feelings that give us pleasure can cause us pain because of the second mark of existence—impermanence, *anicca*. As hard as we look, we can find nothing in the world that is not subject to change. Good, bad, or indifferent, nothing lasts. We know this but have a hard time accepting it, so we grieve anew at each loss. We even forget that impermanence has an upside: just as pleasure doesn't last, neither does pain.

The third kind of suffering is what the Buddha called pervasive suffering (*samkhara-dukkha*), the suffering of conditioned states. This is the suffering we experience by virtue of being born human and caught up in samsara, cyclic existence. Suffering, in this sense, is existential—it's the full catastrophe of being alive for the unenlightened.

Dukkha is not the fate of an unfortunate few. We all experience it until awakening brings relief or transforms our experience of it. In the meantime, knowing that others suffer just as we do can arouse our compassion. Suffering can also be a strong incentive to change. After all, it was confronting the anguish of old age, sickness, and death that knocked Siddhartha Gautama off his gilded perch and set him on the path to enlightenment and the end of suffering.

THE SECOND NOBLE TRUTH: There is a cause of suffering.

The origin of suffering is self-centered craving, the Buddha said. This is not the same as positive desire—the motivation to awaken, for example. Craving (*tanha*, in Pali, *trishna* in Sanskrit) is thirst—insatiable desire that begets more desire. This is the torment of addiction: we get what we want only to want more.

Our craving extends beyond sense pleasures. It is a thirst for existence itself. "As long as there is this 'thirst' to be and to become, the cycle of continuity (*samsara*) goes on," the scholar and monk Walpola Rahula writes in *What the Buddha Taught.* What fuels the suffering of craving is ego, a sense of having an autonomous entity I call *me.* This is a mistaken assumption, the Buddha tells us. The third mark of existence—*anatta*, non-self or selflessness—is that there is no permanent, identifiable entity I can point to as *me. Self* is just a convenient way to label the compound of aggregates, or *skandhas,* that come together when certain causes and conditions arise.

Non-self can be a crushing thought. Our whole worldview is organized around the idea of an enduring self. But insisting on a self that's fixed and unchanging is the ego's eye view and unrealistic. Clinging to wrong ideas about self only brings us pain.

THE THIRD NOBLE TRUTH: There is an end to suffering.

But all is not lost, the Buddha tells us. There is a way through, an end to suffering. It requires investigating our attachments and becoming willing to release them. When we understand the nature of our suffering and see its causes clearly, we become open to seeing truth. Then there is freedom ahead.

THE FOURTH NOBLE TRUTH: There is a way of practice to end suffering.

We want an end to suffering, we have assurance that it's possible, and we have the willingness to pursue it. The question is how? The Buddha understood the challenge of releasing deep-rooted habits, cherished ideas, and self-concern—and he knew well that no external force can release them for us. Ending suffering is inner work—a shift of mind and heart. The Buddha described his own enlightenment: "Vision arose, insight arose, discernment arose, knowledge arose, illumination arose in me with regard to things never heard before."

The Noble Eightfold Path is the way to freedom that the Buddha found. The eight stations along it are stepping-stones to liberation from ignorance, hatred, and the tyranny of self. In Mahayana Buddhism, the view is that we are already enlightened, but our wrong thinking and defilements obscure our Buddha nature. Practicing the Eightfold Path allows us to uncover our inherent goodness.

The Noble Eightfold Path

The Noble Eightfold Path is a training map. For ease of practice, the eight factors are grouped into three categories: Wisdom (*panna*), which encompasses Right View and Right Aspiration; Ethics (*sila*), consisting of Right Speech, Right Action, and Right Livelihood; and Concentration (*samadhi*), comprising Right Effort, Right Mindfulness, and Right Concentration. *Right* in this context is not used in the sense of good versus evil. It refers to the understanding, behavior, and values that point us in the best direction to achieve awakening.

The eight factors do not have to be practiced in a particular order, we are told. They are not meant to be mastered in sequence like the steps of a twelve-step program. The eight points of training are interwoven and mutually supportive. Ideally, we will be working with all of them, more or less simultaneously. But where to start? The Wisdom group develops an understanding and overview of the teachings that provides a firm foundation for deepening meditation practice. Conversely, contemplative practice develops a stable mind that is a base for deeper understanding of the teachings. Ethical conduct helps us develop a sense of inner trustworthiness that supports the whole enterprise.

Wherever you start, practice with diligence. "The Buddha insisted his followers engage with the teachings, both intellectually and experientially," Buddhist scholar and teacher Andrew Olendzki emphasizes. Reading about the Noble Eightfold Path is fine as an introduction, but like any of the Buddha's teachings, to be transformative these practices have to be lived.

WISDOM

Right View, or Right Understanding, means insight into the teachings beyond a mere intellectual grasp. The Vipassana teacher Jack Kornfield describes developing Right View as a two-part task. The first is an inquiry of the heart. "Right understanding starts by acknowledging the suffering and difficulties of the world around us, as well as in our own lives. Then it asks us to touch what we really value inside, to find what we really care about and to use that as the basis of our spiritual practice." The second part, Kornfield says, is to understand how karma works and recognize its transformative power.

Right Aspiration, also called Right Thought, Right Resolve, or Right Intention, involves examining our motivations and making sure we have the energy and perseverance to follow through on our spiritual commitment. For practitioners in the Mahayana tradition, right aspiration is likely to be altruistic: cultivating *bodhicitta,* the compassionate desire to seek awakening for the benefit of all beings.

ETHICS

Ethical conduct was of great importance to the Buddha. It is the foundation of wisdom and compassion, the two wings of Buddhist teaching and practice. A commitment to not harming others is more important than ever today when basic decency is losing ground. Thoughtless, uncaring behavior creates negative karma, the Buddha said.

Right Speech calls for keeping our communications free of lying and gossip and hurtful words. Most of us don't need to think hard to remember a conversation that turned hostile or a verbal exchange that was more divisive than unifying. Every day we have ample opportunities to practice right speech. In the Buddha's day, all communication was oral. For us, it is essential to monitor written communications as well. This is particularly crucial on social media, where anonymity feeds the temptation to misspeak. We have seen how ill-considered or venomous posts can destroy lives and reputations.

Right Action offers more opportunities for monitoring our behavior. When we are fully present, we can see our intentions clearly. If we err or act carelessly, we can deal with it immediately and commit to doing better in the future. A hot button today is sexual conduct. We need to make sure our behavior is respectful, mutual, and not exploitive.

Right Livelihood calls for ethical means of earning a living, including occupations that support the health and well being of society and individuals. Buddhist teaching precludes work that could cause harm, such as manufacturing or selling firearms or anything composed of animal products. If, for example, your business is designing clothing or producing handbags, you could substitute manmade materials for leather and fur. (It has worked out just fine for British fashion designer Stella McCartney, an animal rights advocate.)

CONCENTRATION

Buddhist practice centers on mind training. Meditation opens us to understanding deeper truths. Buddhism has developed many different technologies for training the mind.

Right Effort involves finding a balance between overintensity and laxity in practice, while guarding against unwholesome mind states that get in the way of meditation.

Right Mindfulness refers to maintaining alert, watchful attention to present-moment experience. As the core practice for seeing into the true nature of things, the Buddha taught the Four Foundations of Mindfulness—meditating on: the body (*kaya*); feelings or sensations (*vedana*); mind or mental states (*citta*), and phenomena or mental objects (*dhammas*). The practice associated with this factor is **Vipassana,** which develops insight.

Right Concentration refers to meditation practice that promotes one-pointed concentration and calm abiding (*shamatha*). Through concentration practices, we curb restlessness and develop the ability to sustain attention in all areas of life. **Shamatha** is often practiced in conjunction with Vipassana, or Insight meditation.

The Three Marks of Existence

The Three Marks of Existence—suffering (*dukkha*), non-self (*anatta*), and impermanence (*anicca*)—are the dominant characteristics of samsara, the endless cycle of life, death, and rebirth that is ordinary reality as we experience it. Singly and together, they underlie much of the suffering we experience.

DUKKHA

As noted earlier, dukkha, the first mark of existence, is generally translated as suffering or pain. Other more evocative and more precise translations include unsatisfactoriness, dissatisfaction, stress, sorrow, distress, disappointment, and anguish. Whatever name we give it, it is a pervasive quality of ordinary life, the Buddha taught. It's not that he was opposed to enjoying life. Everyone wants to be happy, as the Dalai Lama always says. The Buddha's concern was that what we usually think of as happiness is only temporary and not true happiness—the joy of an awakened mind. "In Buddhism, happiness is not just a positive feeling but also a state of true freedom from suffering and its causes," the Dalai Lama explains in *From Here to Enlightenment*. "Happiness is deep mental satisfaction that arises from awareness, from wisdom."

IMPERMANENCE

The second mark of existence is impermanence (*anicca* in Pali; *anitya* in Sanskrit). Buddhist teachings say that it is the nature of all compounded or conditioned things—objects and thoughts we experience as real—to decay. Physical or emotional, seen or unseen, nothing lasts. Thoughts and things arise because certain causes and conditions come together, and they disappear when causes and conditions change.

NON-SELF

Non-self, not-self, selflessness (*anatta* in Pali; *anatman* in Sanskrit) is the third mark of existence. This is a difficult concept for us to grasp, because what could be more central to us than our self-identity? Without my personal pronouns, I-me-mine, how do I affirm my existence? How do I relate to the world? Non-self is so challenging to accept because it goes against both our internal experience and our experience of the external world. If there is no *I*, who have I been carrying around all these years? Who laughs and loves and makes decisions?

The Buddha never actually said there is no self. Nor did he say there *is* a self. What he meant by non-self is that there is no eternal soul, no separate permanently existing, intrinsic entity we can definitively identify as *me*. The false belief in an autonomous self is the source of craving, hatred, pride, jealousy, and conceit, we are told. And its effect is far reaching. The Theravadan monk Walpole Rahula, in his classic book *What the Buddha Taught*, calls the idea of self "the source of all the troubles in the world from personal conflict to war between nations. In short, to this false view can be traced all the evil in the world." We cling to the notion of self, Rahula says, out of "deep-rooted" but misguided psychological needs for "self-protection and self-preservation." The Buddha knew well how attached we are to our "ignorance, weakness, fear, and desire," Rahula adds. That was precisely why he decided to show a way to enlightenment that would destroy them at their root.

The Five Aggregates

What we call *self* is a convenience for walking around in the world, a label for the five skandhas—the aggregates or bundles of energy that together make up a human. There's a story from an early Buddhist text, the *Milindapanha* (The Questions of Milinda) that Buddhist teachers often tell to illustrate the concept of non-self. A Buddhist monk, Nagasena, is trying to help King Milinda understand that there is no permanently existing self or soul. When the king asks his name, the monk says he is called Nagasena, but that is merely an identifying label. There is no entity that is Nagasena. The king insists there is, finally asking in frustration, "Is there *anything* apart from the five aggregates that is Nagasena?" When the monk again says no, the king accuses him of lying and demands, "Who, then, do we see before us?" Nagasena decides to try another tack. He asks the king to explain what a chariot is. What part makes it a chariot?

Is it the wheels? The axle? The frame? The pole? The yoke? Nagasena names each piece of the chariot in turn, and each time the King says no, that's not the chariot. "In that case," Nagasena tells him, "I can discover no chariot. It's a lie to say there's a chariot." The King insists, "No, I'm *not* lying. It's *because* of having all those things—the pole, the axle, the wheels, the yoke, the spokes, and so forth—that we call it by a label everyone agrees on: *chariot*." "Very good!" Nagasena tells him. "Your majesty has rightly grasped the meaning of chariot."

Like the chariot, the self is made up of components that individually do not constitute a whole being. Only when they come together in relationship do they form what we label *self*. *Skandha* (*khanda* in Pali) literally means "heap" or "bundle." *Self* is our label for the five heaps or aggregates that comprise what we think of as *myself*. The aggregates are:

Matter (*rupa*), or material form. This includes the six sense organs (eye, ear, nose, tongue, body, and mind—yes, mind is a sense organ in Buddhism) and the objects in the external world that they perceive: visible forms, sounds, smells, tastes, tactile sensations, and thoughts.

Feeling (*vedana*), or sensation. When a sense organ makes contact with an object, sensation arises. It may be pleasant, unpleasant, or neutral.

Perceptions (*samjna*, Sanskrit; *sanna*, Pali). Perceptions recognize things—physical or mental—and label them. They may be accurate or inaccurate in their identification.

Formations (*samskara*, Sanskrit; *sankhara*, Pali). Also known as fabrications, samskara are mental states that lead to volitional action that may be good, bad, or neutral. Only volitional action produces karma, the Buddha said; feelings and perceptions are not karma-producing. Formations include such factors as will, attention, concentration, fear, desire, hate, ignorance, and diligence.

Consciousness (*vijnana*, Sanskrit; *vinnana*, Pali). Consciousness is awareness of the presence of an object without recognizing what it is. Perception is required for recognition.

So how do these processes work together to produce what we think of as a self having an experience of the world? Let's say you're walking on a path in your yard. The sense organ (your eyes, with their capacity for vision) makes contact with (sees) an object lying on the ground. Consciousness makes you aware of the object, but it takes perception to identify it as a snake. With that, an unpleasant sensation arises, followed by a mental formation—a conditioned response of fear, which prompts a volitional action: running away. But let's say the object is *not* a snake, and perception correctly identifies it as a rope. In that case, the formation will not be fear but attention, perhaps, and even diligence, which might prompt the action of leaning down and picking up the rope.

Like the constituent parts of the chariot, when the skandhas arise together, they constitute what we label *self*. But that "self" lacks any inherent, permanent existence. These processes exist only in relationship with one another, and they are continually in flux—arising, stabilizing, decaying, and dissolving.

Karma

Karma is the law of causality. The Buddha didn't invent it; karma is a natural law that says every action has a cause and produces an effect. And every cause is itself the result of the cause that preceded it. The chain of causation governs samsara—everyday, cyclical reality as we perceive it.

In talking about karma, we often confuse the result—which may be good or bad, pleasant or unpleasant—with the action. Karma becomes a moral or ethical issue when we talk about intention or motivation. What we do matters, but in Buddhism an action is said to produce karma only if it is intentional. Doing something unknowingly, with no intention to harm, leaves no blot on your karmic scorecard. But if you think, *I'm going to get back at that so-and-so!* and then you do it, yes, there will be a negative karmic result.

Not all karmic results—*karmic formations* in Buddhist jargon—are negative or unpleasant, of course. The Buddha distinguished between unwholesome karma—motivated by greed, anger, or delusion—and wholesome karma, action that springs from motivations like generosity, kindness, and wisdom. When we do good things, especially caring things that benefit others, we benefit as well. In traditional Buddhist terms, doing good deeds is called "making merit." We don't have to feed orphans in war-torn areas or rescue kittens from burning buildings to make merit. A simple act like watering a neighbor's plants or creating a friendly atmosphere at work also generates a positive result.

The Zen master Dogen urged us to "secretly do good when no one is watching, and if you do wrong, you should confess and repent. In this way good acts done in secret will be rewarded. Open confession of wrongdoing removes the crime so that benefits naturally accrue in this present world and in future worlds."

Geshe Sonam Rinchen, a much-beloved Tibetan Buddhist teacher who died in 2013, claimed that just looking at an image of the Buddha when we are angry can purify eons of negative karma. (It might keep us from acting rashly in the short term, at least.)

Karma reminds us that we are responsible for our lives. As the Buddha stated, "I am the owner of actions (*kamma*), heir to actions, born of actions, related through actions, and have actions as my arbitrator. Whatever I do, for good or for evil, to that will I fall heir."

We may not always see karmic results. They may not even surface in our lifetime. But Buddhism emphasizes the interdependence of all things. Therefore, each of us has a responsibility to the greater good—not just responsibility to family or community or country but to all beings everywhere and to the earth itself. We have no idea how far the results of our actions might reach, so it's wise to assume that they will be far-reaching and therefore to act with integrity. (The Native American Seventh Generation philosophy holds that decisions taken now should be sustainable for seven generations in the future.)

The Bodhisattva Vow—the Mahayana aspiration to awaken

in order to benefit all beings—leaves no room for discrimination, for deciding, *I'll consider this person but not that one. I'll look after the oceans but not the air.* We do not have to actively support every cause; no one has that kind of time or energy. The teachings merely tell us not to close our hearts. At the very least, we can do *metta* meditation (see page 133) for an individual or species that is suffering or in trouble.

No discrimination does not mean no discernment. Setting boundaries, saying no, or exercising tough love is far more compassionate than enabling someone to continue being abusive or self-destructive. Helping for the wrong reasons or jumping in where we are not qualified isn't compassion: it's ego-indulgence. Compassion must be coupled with wisdom. Wisdom and compassion are the two wings of Buddhism. Without both, like a bird, we can't fly.

Samsara and Nirvana

Samsara is day-to-day life as we perceive it. It runs on the causal principle of karma and the twelve links of dependent origination (see page 78). Karma keeps us lashed to the wheel of samsara, to the wash-rinse-repeat cycle of birth, death, and rebirth that continues lifetime after lifetime unless checked. The beginningless and endless round is the pervasive suffering referenced in the Four Noble Truths. The Buddha found a way to stop the merry-go-round and get off for good, but disappearing altogether in parinirvana is not everyone's destination.

Generally speaking, nirvana remains the goal in Buddhism. But nirvana is not a place; it is a state of mind. The word *nirvana* is often defined as "extinguishing" or "blowing out," an extinguishing of craving and aversion, and release from the cycle of rebirth—samsara. But another way of seeing nirvana is as the end of ignorance about the true nature of reality. In the Mahayana view, nirvana is not an escape from samsara but the realization that samsara *is* nirvana. Samsara and nirvana are one. "Nirvana is not something transcendental . . . which stands above this world of birth and death, joy and sorrow, love and hate, peace and struggle," D. T. Suzuki tells us in *Outlines of Mahayana Buddhism*. "Nirvana is not to be sought in the heavens nor after a departure from this earthly life nor in the annihilation of human passions and aspirations. On the contrary it must be sought in the midst of worldliness, as life with all its thrills of pain and pleasure is no more than Nirvana itself."

Our misguided view of nirvana is expressed by the eighteenth-century CE Rinzai Zen master Hakuin Ekaku Zenji in "The Song of Zazen":

> *Not knowing how near the Truth is,*
> *We seek it far away—what a pity!*
> *We are like one who, in the midst of water,*
> *Cries in thirst so imploringly.*

The defilements, the craving, aversion, and ignorance that prevent us from seeing the truth, are not inherent and therefore are impermanent. When we understand this, rather than trying to get rid of them, meditation practice allows us to see their empty nature. The truth, then, is as close as the mind. "To search for enlightenment or nirvana beyond this mind is impossible," we read in *The Zen Teaching of Bodhidharma*, the First Zen Patriarch. "The reality of your own self-nature, the absence of cause and effect, is what's meant by mind. Your mind is nirvana. You might think you can find a buddha or enlighten-ment somewhere beyond the mind, but such a place does not exist."

In discovering our Buddha nature, we understand the paradox that the conditioned mind of suffering and the awak-ened mind (nirvana) are not separate but one.

Dependent Origination

The Buddha's teaching on dependent origination (*paticcasamup-pada* in Pali; *pratityasamutpada* in Sanskrit) is central in all three traditions—Theravada, Mahayana, and Vajrayana. Variously translated as dependent origination, co-dependent origination, conditioned existence, dependent arising, conditioned arising, endless rebirth, and the wheel of suffering, by any name it describes the interconnectedness of conditioned existence, of samsara, establishing that all phenomena are empty of inherent existence, arising only out of the interdependence of their parts. The principle of dependent origination is expressed in the phrase: "When this is, that is. From the arising of this comes the arising of that. When this is not, that is not. With the ces-sation of this comes the cessation of that."

How does this affect us? Dependent origination describes the cycle of birth, death, and rebirth, but more significantly to our sense of well-being as individuals, it outlines step by step the process by which our day-to-day suffering arises.

The twelve links, or *nidanas*, of dependent origination are often depicted graphically in a *bhavachakra,* or wheel. *Bhava* in both Pali and Sanskrit means "existence" or "becoming," while *chakra* is the Sanskrit term for "circle" or "wheel." Illustrating the whole realm of samsaric existence from which we seek liberation, these wheels often appear as intricately detailed and colorful images in Tibetan Buddhist *thangkas*—scroll paintings used as meditative objects. It is traditional for every Tibetan Buddhist monastery to have a wall hanging or mural of the wheel of life in its vestibule.

Graphic depiction of dependent arising is said to have been inspired by the Buddha's solution to a problem King Bimbisara presented to him. The story is that the king received a jewel-studded robe from another ruler, King Udayana, who lived far away. Bimbisara wanted to send Udayana a gift of equal value, but the robe was priceless, and he couldn't think how to match it. *Why not send King Udayana a picture of the Buddha?* his ministers suggested. Painters were summoned, but they were unable to capture the Buddha's image. So the Buddha cast his shadow on a piece of cloth and told the painters to fill in the outline with colors. Then he instructed them to paint at the bottom of the canvas the twelve links of dependent origination in order and in reverse, and across the top of the cloth, some verses. (The progression of the twelve links depicts what binds us to cyclic existence—to the suffering of samsara and the inevitability of rebirth. The links in reverse describe the "unbinding"—the steps to enlightenment, which frees us from the suffering of cyclic existence and the inevitability of rebirth.)

The painting was then wrapped in silks and brocades, placed in a gold box, and dispatched to King Udayana. Bimbisara sent a message telling the king he was about to receive an extraordinary gift and should greet its arrival ceremoniously. Udayana was so annoyed by the command that he was set to wage war on Bimbisara. However, his ministers persuaded him to open the gift first.

The entire court watched breathlessly as the king opened the box and took out the scroll. When he unrolled it, they saw a beautiful portrait—of a complete stranger. Luckily, at court that day were some merchants who recognized the Buddha and spoke of him with great reverence. That night the king took the painting to his quarters. Examining the images carefully and reading the verses, he contemplated the twelve stages of dependent origination going forward and in reverse. He achieved enlightenment and later became a monk.

It's unclear whether the Buddha had the links of dependent origination painted as a circular image on King Bimbisara's gift to King Udayana. But the possibility has spawned countless renderings of the Wheel of Samsara, or Wheel of Life, in the millennia since. The images may differ but the iconography stays much the same. At the hub of the wheel is a circle containing three animals—a cock, a pig, and a snake—representing the three root *kleshas*, the Three Poisons. The cock (attachment) is biting the tail of the snake (aversion); the snake is biting the tail of the pig (ignorance); and the pig is biting the tail of the cock. The kleshas are locked together, inseparable.

Moving out from the center, the next circle is divided in two. On the white side are individuals who have done good deeds ascending to the heavenly realms; on the black side are those who have done bad things and are falling to the hell realms. This imagery is reminiscent of the Buddha's vision on the night of his enlightenment, when he saw beings being

BHAVACHAKRA

THE WHEEL OF LIFE, OR WHEEL OF SAMSARA

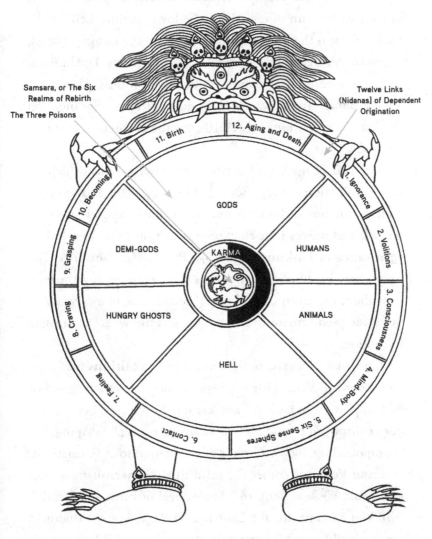

Samsara, or The Six
Realms of Rebirth

The Three Poisons

Twelve Links
(Nidanas) of Dependent
Origination

11. Birth

12. Aging and Death

1. Ignorance

10. Becoming

2. Volitions

9. Grasping

GODS

KARMA

HUMANS

3. Consciousness

DEMI-GODS

8. Craving

HUNGRY GHOSTS

ANIMALS

4. Mind-Body

HELL

7. Feeling

5. Six Sense Spheres

6. Contact

reborn in favorable or unfavorable realms according to their karma.

The third circle from the center is divided into six sections, one for each realm of rebirth. In the lower realms, hell, or the *narak* realm, is the lowest. Just above it are the hungry ghosts, the *pretas*. Above them is the animal, or *tiryag* realm. The human, or *manusya* realm, is the lowest of the upper realms. Above that are the demigods, or *asuras*, and the gods, or *devas*. (For more on the karmic conditions for rebirth, see the **Rebirth** section on page 85.)

The rim of the wheel is where the twelve links of dependent origination are represented. The cycle starts in the upper right at the one o'clock position or in the lower left at seven o'clock and moves in a clockwise direction. The first link is **Ignorance** or **Unknowing** (*avijja,* Pali; *avidya,* Sanskrit). The figure here is a blind person with a cane, representing cluelessness about the truth of suffering. Indeed, lack of awareness of our basic predicament in life is what sets the wheel of samsara in motion.

Ignorance gives rise to the second link, **Volitions** (*sankhara,* Pali; *samskara,* Skt.). This is where intentional actions, good or bad, appear—the fruit of past karma. The image here is of a potter throwing pots. *Sankhara* means "forming," "shaping," or "compounding," so this link is often referred to as Formations.

From Volitions comes the third link, **Consciousness** (*vinnana,* Pali; *vijnana,* Skt.). In "The Wheel of Birth and Death," Bhikkhu Khantipalo, aka Laurence Mills, a Western Buddhist teacher and former Theravadan monk, calls this "relinking-consciousness"—consciousness arising from a previous lifetime. This is consciousness that carries karmic imprints and is primed for rebirth in samsara. The image is of a monkey. In some versions, it is a playful monkey, attracted by the shiny objects of samsara; in others, it is a monkey eating fruit—the fruit of past karma.

Consciousness gives rise to the fourth link, **Mind–Body** (*nama-rupa,* Pali/Skt.), often known as **Name and Form**. In Buddhism, earthly life is said to begin here. The image is of a boat with a pilot and passengers. Bhikkhu Khantipalo suggests that the pilot represents the mind, propelling "the boat of psychophysical states on the river of cravings, while body is the passive passenger."

From mind-body arises the fifth link, the **Six Sense Spheres** (*ayatana,* Pali.; *shadayatana,* Skt.). The usual image for this link is a house with six windows or five windows and a door. The openings represent the six senses—eyes, ears, nose, tongue, touch, and mind—which receive information via sense objects: sights, sounds, smells, tastes, touchable things, and thoughts. The mind collects and processes all this information, adding memories from the past, thoughts about the present, and hopes or fears for the future.

From the Six Sense Spheres arises the sixth link, **Contact** (*phassa,* Pali; *sparsha,* Skt.). The image here is of a couple kissing or making love. When the senses are open and oriented toward an object, contact is made.

From Contact, **Feeling** *(vedana,* Pali/Skt.), or **Sensation,** the seventh link, arises. Sensations in Buddhism are of three kinds: pleasant, unpleasant, or neutral. The image of a man blinded by an arrow conveys the idea that in a world of impermanence, happiness based on pleasant feelings can't be counted on to last.

From Feeling, the eighth link, **Craving** (*tanha,* Pali; *trishna,* Skt.), or **Thirst**—clinging to sensation—arises. Up to now, the links have been based on past karma. Craving brings us into the present, where we create new karma, Bhikkhu Khantipalo says. The image is of a man drinking alcohol. Khantipalo recommends that we engage in practice, especially mindfulness, so we won't "be swept away by the force of past habits and let craving and unknowing increase" in our hearts. Mindfulness of feelings will increase our awareness of the Three Poisons, he says, and with this knowledge, we can "break out of the wheel of birth and death." Without practice, feelings will just lead to more craving and "whirl one around this wheel full of dukkha."

From Craving arises the ninth link, **Grasping** (*upadana,* Pali/Skt.), **Clinging,** or **Attachment**. This is craving intensified and diversified, according to Bhikkhu Khantipalo. Here the threat is not only lusting after sensual pleasures but also falling away from the Dharma and adopting wrong views, such as belief in a permanently existing soul. The image, of a monkey grabbing all the fruit off a tree, suggests that when craving reaches this point, our response is to grab even more, mistakenly thinking that more will bring happiness.

Grasping gives rise to the tenth link, **Becoming** (*bhava,* Pali/Skt.). "With hearts boiling with craving and grasping," as Bhikkhu Khantipalo puts it, all the brakes are off in the push for existence. Not understanding how dukkha works, we add fuel to the fire rather than arresting craving and grasping, "and cutting [ignorance] off at its root." Recommitting to Dharma practice "will contribute to whatever we become, or do not become, at the end of this life," Bhikkhu Khantipalo says. The image for this link, appropriately, is of a pregnant woman.

Becoming is followed by **Birth** (*jati,* Pali/Skt.), the eleventh link. The image is of a woman giving birth. The issue here is, will we be able to get off the wheel of samsara or will we be doomed to another round? Whatever future awaits us will be conditioned by the karma arising in this lifetime.

Where there is birth, **Aging and Death** (*jara-marana,* Pali; *jaramaranam,* Skt.) inevitably follow. In the twelfth link, the image is of a corpse being carried to the cemetery. If we haven't done the work, haven't committed to releasing wrong views and destructive patterns and emotions, our future will be "lives without end but also deaths without end," warns Bhikkhu Khantipalo. Here, the imagery signifies not just death but decay and the suffering of constant change. The way off the wheel, the Buddha taught, is the dharma path, which leads to nirvana, beyond all suffering.

Often, the wheel is pictured clamped in the jaws of a fearsome wrathful deity, Yama the Lord of Death, a vivid symbol of impermanence. Above the wheel is often an image of the Buddha pointing to the moon—symbol of nirvana, of liberation.

Just how important the Buddha considered the teachings on dependent origination is expressed in a line from the Salistamba Sutra (Rice Seedling Scripture): "Whoever . . . sees conditioned arising sees Dharma, and whoever sees Dharma sees the Buddha."

Rebirth

Karma is one of the five facts of life we should reflect on often, the Buddha said. The other four? Aging, sickness, death, and being separated from all that is dear to us. According to Buddhist teachings, the karmic consequences of our actions extend beyond the here and now. Past karma followed us into this lifetime. And whatever karma we now accrue will follow us into the next life, affecting the nature of our rebirth.

Rebirth is a core teaching of Buddhism, but for many Westerners, it is a stumbling block to fully embracing Buddhist practice. The Abrahamic religions—Christianity, Judaism, and Islam—believe in an afterlife where we're rewarded or punished for our behavior on earth. But that's where it ends. We resist the idea of rebirth or karma that extends from lifetime to lifetime.

According to Buddhist teachings, rebirth is inevitable for the unenlightened. As long as we continue in cyclic existence, accumulated karma will determine the kind of death we will have as well as the kind of rebirth. The Theravadan teaching is that rebirth occurs soon after dying. The Tibetan Buddhist view is that after death, the deceased spends forty-nine days in the *bardo*, a transitional state between death and rebirth. *The Tibetan Book of the Dead* contains elaborate instructions and rituals to help with the passage. Consciousness at the time of death is said to influence the deceased's experience in the bardo, as well as the conditions of rebirth. The teachings in *The Tibetan Book of the Dead* are considered valuable advice for experiencing a good life as well as a good death.

According to Buddhist cosmology, karmic debt from previous lifetimes along with karma earned in the most recent lifetime heavily influence the realm into which we will be reborn. (Sounds a bit like the Hogwarts sorting hat assigning wizardry students to their proper houses.) The ultimate goal in Buddhism is not to be reborn at all, but in the meantime the aim is to clear our karma. What's important to remember is that these realms are not physical places but mental states.

The lowest realm, the hell realm, is the repository of those who have committed crimes or broken their vows. The mind state here is hatred. The teachings say there are eighteen different hells (*narakas*), plunging the unfortunate who land here into teeth-chattering cold and blazing heat, and tormenting them with unceasing attacks and visions of respite that are out of reach. Beings here endure unspeakable torture until they have worked off enough unfavorable karma to earn a more propitious rebirth. That could take many lifetimes, it is said, as surviving the continual assault leaves no time for practice.

A step up is the realm of the hungry ghosts, the pretas. The hungry ghosts have huge stomachs and tiny mouths: they are perpetually hungry and thirsty but can never get their fill. This realm is for those who are consumed with greed, attachment, and insatiable desire. The mind state is constant craving.

The animal realm is next, the highest of the lower realms. The mind state here is one of ignorance and confusion. Rebirth in this realm is said to result from ignoring other people's needs. How exactly that squares with the loyalty we experience from our pets is unclear. But if we thought it wouldn't be so bad to be reborn as someone's kitten, we might not be so lucky. Even in the prosperous West, most animals don't have an easy life. You could be a chicken or steer penned up in a factory farm, being force-fed hormones till time for slaughter.

Above the animals is the human realm, where beings are still attached to the three root poisons, plus envy and pride. Rebirth in the human realm is considered the most desirable, as it offers the best opportunity and greatest incentive for achieving enlightenment and release from rebirth. Having been human before, we know the drill, and presumably could do better this time.

Above the human realm are the demigods, where jealousy is the prevailing state of mind. Beings who land here had good intentions in their previous lifetime but failed miserably on follow-through. The demigods possess godlike qualities, but they continue to accumulate karma through their petty squabbling.

Good behavior will get you into the highest realm, that of the gods, or devas, but it may not be such a blessing in the end. The mind state here is pride. And the god realm is said to be so blissful and pleasure filled that beings here are too attached to worldly delights to engage in the spiritual practice necessary to work off karma.

All very interesting, but for some of us the obvious question is: If there is no self, what is it that is reborn? The Buddha declined to answer this and other questions about the self, on the grounds that such discussion wouldn't lead to awakening. Other Buddhist teachers are vague on the subject of what is reborn. The prevailing Buddhist view seems to be that *self* is merely a label for what the Dalai Lama describes as "a complex flow of mental and physical events, clustered in clearly identifiable patterns." This definition precludes the notion of continuity of consciousness from one lifetime to the next. But that doesn't quite square with the elaborate bardo teachings in *The Tibetan Book of the Dead*, or, for that matter, the tulku tradition in Tibetan Buddhism. A tulku is a lama believed to incarnate with the "mindstream" of a high teacher from a previous lifetime.

There *are* Buddhists who argue for some form of continuity— at the very least, a *seed* of consciousness or a karmic imprint carried from one lifetime to the next. To understand rebirth and cultivate compassion, Buddhist students are often given the practice of recognizing that every sentient being in the universe has been your mother in a previous lifetime. It starts with accepting that the stream of consciousness that was present at your birth arose from the consciousness of the birth before that and the one before that, and so on back to infinity. "If the continuity of mind is beginningless, we must have taken countless rebirths and therefore must have had countless mothers," Geshe Kelsang Gyatso explains in *Meaningful to Behold: The Bodhisattva's Way of Life*. This may not answer the question of what is reborn, but at least the practice opens our hearts to compassion for our fellow beings in this lifetime.

The Three Poisons

Poisons. Ominous sounding. And considering the destructive role played by the Three Poisons—attachment, aversion, and ignorance—poison isn't a bad way to characterize them. Also called afflictions or defilements, they are the Big Three destructive mind states that keep us spinning in samsara day after day and lifetime after lifetime. You could call them the root of all evil.

If one of the triplets has precedence over the others, it is ignorance. Deluded thinking, lack of understanding, is the *root* root—the clouded mind that obscures our view of the true nature of things, allowing destructive emotions to run riot.

Not that the Three Poisons—*kleshas* in Sanskrit—are the only mind states responsible for unwholesome choices. In the Mahayana tradition, pride and envy join the list. And the Yogacara

school of Mahayana Buddhism identifies six root kleshas—
the Big Three plus pride, doubt, and wrong view—saying they
arise because of our wrong view of self, our insistence on an
independently existing *I*.

The Eight Worldly Conditions

Life in samsara is "just one thing after another," as one Buddhist
teacher often jokes. Inevitably it's the good mixed with the
bad. Unless we develop equanimity, the Buddha said, we will
continue to be tossed around by the vicissitudes of life: "eight
worldly conditions that keep the world turning around and
that the world turns around." What are the eight? Gain and
loss, fame and disrepute, praise and blame, pleasure and pain.

Given their impermanent nature, it is easy to see how even
favorable conditions can let us down. When we truly understand the transient nature of life, the Buddha said, we will no
longer make distinctions about worldly conditions. Accepting
what is will liberate us from suffering.

The Precepts

From the beginning, the precepts, as spelled out in the Vinaya,
played a crucial role in Buddhism, ensuring the harmonious
functioning of the sangha and facilitating practice on the path
to enlightenment. The precepts are not commandments handed
down from on high, as in many religions. The rules for the
monks evolved over time, with the Buddha only adding them
as needed to resolve disputes among the monks and provide
guidelines for his lay followers.

For us, the precepts bring the teachings alive in daily life. They not only offer training in self-discipline and refraining from destructive behavior but also encourage development of positive qualities like kindness and generosity. At the deepest level, practicing the precepts brings us ever closer to the true happiness of awakening.

"The Buddhist precepts are not intended to force us into a particular way of behaving but to encourage us to reflect on our motivations and actions," Martine Batchelor, a former Korean Zen nun and author of *Meditation for Life*, explains in a special section on the precepts in *Tricycle: The Buddhist Review.* "Since the aim of a Buddhist life is to diminish suffering, Buddhist ethics are rooted in compassion and wisdom, and we understand that our intentions and actions have consequences."

Batchelor suggests three different ways of approaching the precepts, based on the different Buddhist traditions. Theravada precepts, grounded in monasticism, are about restraint, she points out, so in some situations, what's required is simply self-discipline. Mahayana precepts focus on intention, so at other times, we might need to look at what behavior would be the most "skillful to alleviate suffering." Tibetan Buddhist precepts reflect the tantric view that good or bad, our behavior can be a vehicle for transformation, Batchelor says. So "sometimes we have to sit with the messiness of our minds and actions and try to transform them from within."

The number of precepts varies by tradition. The Five Lay Precepts are common to all three traditions. They have been described as the "bare minimum" of moral standards in Buddhism, but in the long run, they are so much more. Keeping the precepts nurtures compassion, helps us build better relationships, and moves us closer to awakening.

THE FIVE LAY PRECEPTS

The First Precept: Refrain from Killing

Any sort of injurious behavior toward other living beings runs counter to Buddhist principles. But behavior in Buddhist terms rests on intention, so mindfulness is essential. Inadvertently stepping on an insect would not violate this precept, but smashing it with a flyswatter would. People often talk about seeing monks carefully scooping tiny insects off the floor and depositing them safely in the grass outside. Protecting wildlife and other vulnerable beings, regardless of species, is a very Buddhist thing to do.

Abortion, suicide, and euthanasia are grave acts that inarguably involve killing, and they pose agonizing dilemmas for some Buddhists. Abortion is against the precepts but a choice that circumstances lead some women to make. In Japan, where abortion is legal, there is a beautiful Zen Buddhist ritual of mourning, *mizuko kuyo,* that speaks to the anguish involved in the decision. Offerings are made to Jizo Bosatsu, a Pure Land bodhisattva who relieves suffering and is the protector of aborted, miscarried, and stillborn babies. Some women find closure in placing a small memorial statue, *mizuko jizo,* in a temple or cemetery.

Eating animal products and wearing clothes made of animal hides are other choices that involve destroying living creatures. Although the Buddha was not a vegetarian—he and his monks ate whatever food they received as alms—many Buddhists today maintain a vegetarian or vegan diet to avoid destroying life. To take this precept to the ultimate extreme, you could trace the delivery chain of everything you eat to make sure that no beings were harmed or exploited along the way. A more realistic way to keep the precept is to say a prayer of gratitude for all beings involved in your meal. That would include gratitude to everyone from the cook to the microscopic creatures that were removed from the lettuce before it came to market. At Buddhist retreat centers, participants often chant or recite verses of appreciation at mealtimes.

The benefits of keeping the precept not to kill are clear. Anyone will feel safe in our presence, secure in the knowledge that we will do them no harm.

The Second Precept: Refrain from Taking What Is Not Given

Theft of other people's property in all forms violates this precept. That means no raiding your child's piggy bank for parking-meter change. With theft, as with killing, intention is all. As Bhikkhu Bodhi points out, the world is full of opportunities to violate this precept. Some are seemingly so routine we don't think twice about them, such as taking home a pen or pad from the office. Theft doesn't have to involve loss of money or property to cause pain: think of stealing ideas from a colleague or stealing time from your boss or family and friends.

Insight meditation teacher Donald Rothenberg, author of *The Engaged Spiritual Life,* suggests considering this precept from several perspectives, including weighing the balance of giving and taking in your daily life.

The Third Precept: Refrain from Misusing Sexual Energy

For Buddhist monastics this generally means no sex. For lay practitioners, it means refraining from improper sexual relations. This is a hot topic these days, with so many accusations of sexual misconduct. This precept is an opportunity to monitor your sexual behavior carefully to make sure it is 100 percent consensual, violates no standards of care and decency, and is neither physically nor psychologically harmful or exploitive.

The Fourth Precept: Refrain from Incorrect Speech

The short form of this precept is *no lying,* but lying is only one form of wrong speech. Others the Buddha cited include "divisive speech, abusive speech, and idle chatter." Even that doesn't include the half-truths we tell to get out of sticky situations, exaggerate our accomplishments, or get something we want. The Buddha advised his son, Rahula, to reflect on his words before, during, and after any conversation. False speech creates what the Surangama Sutra refers to as "impure karma of the mouth." Our speech may not always be sweet: sometimes we have to speak truth that is harsh. But even then we need to check our intentions and weigh our words carefully. Our aim should always be to not harm others or say anything we might later regret. There is always that time-honored motherly advice: *If you can't say something nice, don't say anything.*

The Buddha didn't have email and social media to worry about when he drafted the precepts. Or the written word, for that matter. Every caveat about speech should be applied to written communications as well. This precept reminds us to pause before hitting Send and consider the consequences of any words we post on social media.

The Fifth Precept: Abstain from Intoxicants

A clear mind is essential for progressing along the Buddhist path. Alcohol and drugs can cloud our thinking and compromise our ability to concentrate. For this reason, many Buddhist practitioners strictly observe this precept and don't drink or take drugs. A Middle Way view would be to opt for moderation. Even the use of prescription drugs should be examined, in light of the current epidemic of opioid addiction.

The Buddha spoke of "heedlessness" caused by intoxicant use leading to "moral recklessness." Bhikkhu Bodhi reminds us that being under the influence can make us lose control and possibly violate the other four precepts. In *Going for Refuge & Taking the Precepts*, he tells us that following this precept can prevent "the misfortunes that result from the use of intoxicants: loss of wealth, quarrels and crimes, bodily disease, loss of reputation, shameless conduct, negligence, and madness." That's enough to make anyone rethink those pot brownies.

During periods of intense practice, such as meditation retreats, practitioners in the Theravada and Tibetan traditions may abstain from sex altogether and follow three additional precepts: not eating after midday; not sleeping on a high or comfortable bed; and not wearing perfume or jewelry or indulging in dancing, singing, or listening to music.

Novice monks in the Theravada tradition take an additional two vows. In the Tibetan Buddhist tradition, novices adhere to as many as thirty-six precepts.

THE TEN MAJOR BODHISATTVA PRECEPTS

Mahayana Buddhists follow ten major precepts. These are

similar to the Theravadan precepts in that they contain behavior to be avoided, but they also include positive behavior in keeping with the Bodhisattva Vow to help all sentient beings. In the first major precept, for example, the bodhisattva should not only refrain from killing but also nurture a mind of compassion, "always devising expedient means to rescue and protect all beings." And in the eighth major precept—a vow not to be stingy—the bodhisattva should give anyone who asks for help whatever they need. Refusing to give the poor even a coin, a needle, or a blade of grass would be considered a major violation.

The Brahma Viharas

The teachings on the Brahma Viharas—the Four Immeasurables or "boundless states"—are much loved by practitioners in all three Buddhist traditions. *Vihara* means "abode" or "dwelling place," and *brahma* refers to the gods, so the Brahma Viharas are "heavenly abodes" or more loosely, "sublime attitudes" or "sublime states of mind." Dwelling in these four core virtues—loving-kindness, compassion, sympathetic joy, and equanimity—is said to open any heart and transform the fear, indifference, envy, and ill-will that separate us from others and our own Buddha nature.

The Brahma Vihara teachings did not originate with the Buddha. They were drawn from ancient Indian sources, then further developed by the Buddha. The *Karaniya Metta Sutta* (Hymn of Universal Love) is one of the most popular teachings in the Pali canon, and Buddhaghosa devoted a lengthy chapter in the *Visuddhimagga* (The Path of Purification) to practicing the divine abidings. The forest monk Thanissaro Bhikkhu describes the Brahma Viharas as "the Buddha's primary heart teachings—the ones that connect most directly with our desire for true happiness."

Significantly, they also connect us most directly with one another. In *A Heart as Wide as the World*, Sharon Salzberg, who has been teaching the Brahma Viharas in the West for more than forty years, calls them "practices that cultivate our faith in our own loving hearts and the strength of our connection with others."

METTA, LOVING-KINDNESS

Metta, the first of the four Brahma Viharas, is an outpouring of warm-heartedness toward others, a sincere wish for their happiness and well-being. Translated most often as "loving-kindness," it is also known as unconditional friendliness, benevolence, and goodwill. By any name, it is love untainted by self-interest.

Love untainted by self-interest? Is there such a thing? we might wonder. And does it mean that we should always put others before ourselves? The Buddha was astute about human nature, and when questions like that were put to him, his answers were seldom the predictable. One memorable teaching on self-interest was prompted by an exchange between King Pasenadi, one of the Buddha's benefactors and closest disciples, and his wife, Queen Mallika. The king asked her, "Is there anyone dearer to you than yourself?" She replied no and asked him the same question. Pasenadi's answer was also no. Apparently the exchange bothered the king, however, because he went to the Buddha and asked what he thought. All the Buddha said was, "Searching all directions with your awareness, you find no one dearer than yourself. In the same way, others are thickly dear to themselves. So you shouldn't hurt others if you love yourself."

Building on that idea, the Indian monk Acharya Buddharakkhita suggests a way to curb our self-centeredness: "The mind becomes universal by identifying its own interest with the interest of all," he writes in *Metta: The Philosophy and Practice of Universal Love.*

So how do we develop loving-kindness toward all beings? The classic Metta practice on page 133 is a place to start. Acharya Buddharakkhita also proposes meditating on the Buddha's Karaniya Metta Sutta. There's a charming tale in Buddhist lore suggesting how that might work out.

As the story goes, five hundred monks went off to a forest grove to spend the rainy season in meditation. As it happened, the forest was also populated by tree spirits who felt it would be disrespectful for them to live in the trees while the monks were there. They wrongly assumed the monks were just there overnight, and when they found out the monks planned to stay for three months, they were upset. Anxious to get their homes back, the tree spirits began harassing the monks, conjuring ghoulish visions and demonic voices to frighten them off, and inducing sneezing and coughing fits. Finally, the monks gave up and left. They went to the Buddha to complain. To their shock, he told them to return to the forest. "You went there the first time unarmed," he said. "This time you must take a weapon." Puzzled, they asked what sort of weapon. "Just before you enter the forest grove, recite the Metta Sutta," he said. The monks followed his instructions, and they generated so much loving-kindness that the tree spirits welcomed them and became their protectors from then on.

The metta teachings make clear how damaging anger is to ourselves and others. The *Dhammapada,* a much-loved collection of the Buddha's sayings, contains these famous lines, a popular rendering of verse 5: "Hatred never ceases by hatred, but by love alone is healed. This is the ancient and eternal law." Love and hate can't coexist, the *Visuddhimagga* emphasizes. Buddhaghosa devotes seventeen pages of the loving-kindness section to how to get rid of anger and the consequences if we don't. We are given to understand that if we can generate loving-kindness for ourselves, for our loved ones, for people we feel neutral about, and even for our enemies, the results will be nothing short of miraculous. In another Metta scripture, the *Mettanisamsa Sutta* (Discourse on Advantages of Loving-Kindness), the Buddha enumerates the blessings that accrue from cultivating loving-kindness, among them: "You will sleep in comfort, wake in comfort, and have no bad dreams; your mind will be concentrated, nothing will harm you, people will love and protect you—and you will be reborn in one of the god realms."

Even if you are not into the idea of rebirth, there is one teaching in this area that could have a salutary effect on your life here and now. We would be hard-pressed, the Buddha suggested, to find anyone who has not been our mother or father or sibling or child in a previous lifetime. Reflect on that for a while, and it puts a different spin on being angry with that co-worker who never seems to pull his weight.

Loving-kindness practice is said to make the ten perfections, or *paramitas,* come alive in us. These are the Buddha-like qualities we need to develop for awakening. Two of the Brahma

Viharas—loving-kindness and equanimity—are already on the list. The other eight are: generosity, morality, renunciation, wisdom, energy, patience, truthfulness, and determination.

KARUNA, COMPASSION

The second Brahma Vihara is compassion, *karuna*. This is a fervent wish for all beings to be free of suffering. There's nothing shy about this aspiration. When we feel it, we go all in. Compassion "allows us to name injustice without hesitation, and to act strongly, with all the skill at our disposal," Sharon Salzberg writes in *Lovingkindness*. "[It] allows us to bear witness to that suffering, whether it is in ourselves or others, without fear."

The first step to developing a compassionate heart, Salzberg tells us, is "to acknowledge that pain and sorrow exist." We have to be willing to see it, recognize it, and open to it.

Seems simple, but it's not always easy. How often we run the other way, or at least avert our eyes, when someone is in obvious distress. Opening to another person's anguish raises another set of issues. Open without thinking, and compassion may be insincere—crocodile tears. Or what the Tibetan Buddhist tulku Chögyam Trungpa—borrowing a term from Gurdjieff— called *idiot compassion*: doing good but for selfish ends, or not having the guts to say no. Sometimes the most compassionate thing we can do is acknowledge the suffering but *not* step in to help—especially if we're not qualified, or our help is not wanted, or we could actually do harm.

Empathy is the key to compassion. To feel another's pain arouses the wish for their pain to end. To develop compassion,

Buddhaghosa suggests we look for the most wretched, unfortunate person we can find. Failing that, he suggests arousing compassion for an "evil-doing" person, with the aspiration *May you be free of suffering and the causes of suffering.*

But compassion is not just for the down and out. Everyone deserves our compassion, even our enemies. Those who are riding high now may have a turn of fortune. So we should arouse compassion for a person who is dear to us and for an enemy with the same aspiration: *May you be free of suffering and the causes of suffering.*

MUDITA, SYMPATHETIC JOY

The third Brahma Vihara, sympathetic joy or gladness, means rejoicing in others' success and good fortune. This is acknowledged to be the most difficult Brahma Vihara to arouse. We all want the people we love to be happy and achieve their dreams. But when someone we know meets success, there may be a niggling little feeling of jealousy or envy mixed in with our gladness—especially if that person has received or achieved something we dearly wished for ourselves. We may judge the person unworthy of the honor, or think it unfair when others succeed where we have not been successful.

The negative qualities that prevent us from arousing *mudita* "all are rooted in the binding forces of aversion and attachment," Sharon Salzberg points out in *Lovingkindness*, while the qualities that foster it "share their origin in basic goodness." If we're unable to summon sympathetic joy, Salzberg suggests feeling gratitude for what we have. She cites the blessings the Buddha says can be ours if we cultivate gratitude, from work we like and a satisfying home life to patience and good friends.

Tibetan Buddhists approach *empathetic* joy, as they call it, by "rejoicing in virtue, which is the root of happiness," teacher and former monk B. Alan Wallace says. Start by rejoicing in your own good qualities and behavior, he suggests in *The Four Immeasurables: Cultivating a Boundless Heart.* "Recognize that you have done something good and take delight in it."

UPEKKHA, EQUANIMITY

Equanimity, the fourth Brahma Vihara, is substantially different from the other three. While loving-kindness, compassion, and sympathetic joy all *arouse* energy, equanimity is calming. In fact, it is so reserved that it may seem uncaring at first. But it is essential for us to be able to stay calm and balanced when we encounter suffering. A cool head in a tense moment or an emergency may make the difference that saves the situation or even saves a life. Equanimity is the quality we would want in a doctor or nurse: compassionate and sensitive to the patient and the problem but not overidentified or emotionally overwhelmed. An equanimous mother is a blessing for her child, a steady presence when the child has a meltdown.

It is easier, of course, to remain calm in nonthreatening situations and around neutral people, less so when emotions are involved—all the more reason to develop equanimity. The teachings tell us that equanimity is a counterweight to the uncertainty of impermanence, a balancing force in the midst of an ever-shifting world and our ever-changing moods.

THE SECOND TURNING OF THE WHEEL:
MAHAYANA BUDDHISM

Mahayana Buddhism, the "Great Vehicle," has its roots in the sects that split off from Theravada Buddhism following the so-called Great Schism a century or two after the Buddha's death. Mahayana doctrine includes the basic teachings of the Pali Canon: the Four Noble Truths and the Noble Eightfold Path, karma, dependent origination, samsara, and nirvana. Like Theravada Buddhism, Mahayana Buddhism is grounded in the scriptures—*sutras,* in Sanskrit—but the Mahayana canon extends beyond the teachings of the historical Buddha.

The Second Turning of the Wheel of Dharma refers to the Mahayana teachings that took place over a twelve-year period on Vulture Peak outside Rajgir, in Bihar, India. The Buddha is said to have delivered them to an audience of 1,250 bodhisattvas, monks, nuns, and laypersons. The centerpiece of the teachings is the series of **Prajnaparamita (Perfection of Wisdom) sutras**, which focus on *shunyata,* or emptiness, and **bodhicitta**, the compassionate aspiration to awaken for the benefit of all beings. These teachings formed the basis of the Madhyamaka, or Middle Way, school founded by the Indian scholar Nagarjuna, who lived from 150 to 250 CE. They play a significant role in Chan and Zen Buddhism. The most widely known of the Perfection of Wisdom sutras is the **Maha Prajnaparamita Hrdaya Sutra (Great Heart of Perfect Wisdom Scripture)**, the ultimate teaching on emptiness. (For more on the Heart Sutra, see page 108.)

Among other notable Mahayana texts are:

The Lotus Sutra, one of the most significant of the Mahayana sutras. It includes teachings on *upaya,* or skillful means, and universal Buddhahood, the notion that all beings have the potential to become buddhas. Initially, the Buddha taught the Triyana—three possible vehicles for awakening: hearing teachings directly from the Buddha; awakening by one's own effort, such as through meditation; or following the bodhisattva path, seeking enlightenment out of an altruistic desire to help all beings reach nirvana. But in the Lotus Sutra he revises this teaching to say that the three are not separate but constitute one vehicle. Central to the Tendai and Nichiren schools of Japanese Buddhism, the Lotus Sutra is unusual among Mahayana texts for asserting the importance of faith and devotion.

The Lankavitara Sutra ("Scripture of the Descent into Lanka"), a dialogue between the Buddha and the bodhisattva Mahamati ("great wisdom"), set on the island fortress of Lanka. It contains teachings on Buddha nature and the Yogacara doctrine of the eight consciousnesses, including the repository or "storehouse" consciousness. The sutra was influential in the development of Buddhism in China, Japan, and Tibet, particularly Chan and Zen Buddhism.

The Avatamsaka Sutra (Flower Garland Scripture), a long, ornate Chinese text reflecting both Madhyamaka and

Yogacara doctrines. It expands on the notion of Buddha nature and covers such topics as the visionary powers of meditation and the *dharmadhatu*—which here refers to the entire universe, the realm of the Buddha.

The Way of the Bodhisattva

The aspiration in Theravada Buddhism is individual enlightenment—to extinguish suffering and desire and, with the Buddha as a model, be a never-returner. In Mahayana Buddhism, awakening is still important, but the bodhisattva seeks awakening in order to help all beings, vowing to stick around as long as it takes for everyone everywhere to be enlightened. The bodhisattva ideal is one of the core Mahayana teachings. *Bodhi* is Sanskrit for awake, enlightened; *sattva* means consciousness. In the Jataka Tales, stories of the Buddha's past lives, the *Bodhisattva* refers to the Buddha while he was still in Tusita Heaven, the heavenly realm where a bodhisattva destined to become a Buddha hangs out, perfecting himself to be born on earth. In the Mahayana tradition, a bodhisattva is someone who develops bodhicitta, the altruistic aspiration to awaken in order to help all beings. Bodhicitta is often translated as "mind of enlightenment," "awakening mind," or "awakened heart." (The Sanskrit word *citta* means both "mind" and "heart.") It is an expansive quality revealing a deep well of compassion.

There is no creator God in Buddhism, but in Mahayana Buddhism there is a pantheon of bodhisattvas who have realized the ideal and have been elevated to god-like status. The most important of the bodhisattvas is Avalokiteshvara—Chenrezig in Tibetan—the bodhisattva of compassion who assumes female form as Kwan Yin in Chan Buddhism and Kanzeon Bosatsu in Zen. Another key figure is Manjushri, the bodhisattva of wisdom.

But being a bodhisattva isn't just for the gods. It is an aspiration for all. The Bodhisattva Vow is a formal commitment to devote one's life to serving others. Part of that commitment is to perfect the qualities of a Buddha. Though the Mahayana sutras list six basic perfections (*paramitas*)—generosity (*dana*), virtue (*sila*), patience (*ksanti*), diligence (*virya*), concentration (*dhyana*), and wisdom (*prajna*)—the bodhisattva path adds another four: skill in means or discriminating awareness (*upaya*), aspiration (*pranidhana*), spiritual power (*bala*), and knowledge (*jnana*). Chö-gyam Trungpa Rinpoche had this to say about what it means to be a bodhisattva: "Taking the Bodhisattva Vow implies that instead of holding our own individual territory and defending it tooth and nail, we become open to the world that we are living in. It means we are willing to take on greater responsibility . . . Rather than focusing on our own little projects, we expand our vision immensely to embrace working with the rest of the world, the rest of the galaxies, the rest of the universes."

In *No Time to Lose,* Pema Chödrön's guide to *The Way of the Bodhisattva,* a classic work by the eighth century CE Nalanda scholar-monk Shantideva, she outlines three ways of working with the Bodhisattva Vow, depending on our level of commitment. A kingly or queenly approach involves working on ourselves first, in order to awaken so we can best help others. The ferryman approach acknowledges that we're all in the same boat, with the same hindrances, hopes, and fears, so we connect with others through empathy and loving-kindness. The shepherd approach is that of putting the welfare of others before our own.

Most of us think self-sacrifice is the only "real" compassion, Ani Pema notes, and although there will be times when we step up in this way, "to hold this as our only model would definitely be misleading," she says. "Instead, we can proceed at any of the three levels," she suggests. "To awaken bodhicitta we start where we are and go forward step by step."

There are many versions of the Bodhisattva Vow—sometimes referred to as "Great Vows for All"—but they all express the same aspiration. This version is the *Shigu Seigan* (Great Vows for All), from the Zen Studies Society in New York City. It is chanted at morning service at Shobo-ji, the city zendo, and at Dai Bosatsu Zendo Kongo-ji, the mountain monastery in upstate New York.

> *However innumerable all beings are, I vow to save them all.*
> *However inexhaustible delusions are, I vow to extinguish them all.*
> *However immeasurable Dharma teachings are, I vow to master them all.*
> *However endless the Buddha's Way is, I vow to follow it.*

For advanced practitioners or anyone else strongly motivated to cultivate bodhicitta, Rob Preece, a Tibetan Buddhist teacher and psychologist, suggests repeating the Bodhisattva Vow one hundred thousand times as a practice. (Be prepared: it will take you awhile.)

Emptiness

Another core teaching of Mahayana Buddhism is *shunyata*, or emptiness, as elucidated in the Prajnaparamita Sutras (Perfection of Wisdom Scriptures). Shunyata pushes the Theravadan teaching of anatta, or non-self, to the limit, declaring that *all* phenomena are empty of inherent existence, coming into being only as causes and conditions come together in an interdependent universe. The Maha Prajnaparamita Hridaya Sutra (Great Heart of Perfect Wisdom Scripture) is the main text establishing emptiness as ultimate reality. Commonly known as the Heart Sutra, it is one of the most beloved of all the Mahayana sutras and is chanted nearly every day in most Chan and Zen temples.

The doctrine of shunyata (sunnata, Pali), or emptiness, makes no distinction between the everyday world of appearances and ultimate reality. When the Heart Sutra says "Form is emptiness; emptiness is form," it is not a statement of nihilism, saying that nothing exists, the scholar Mu Soeng emphasizes in *The Heart of the Universe.* Shunyata "is simply about 'seeing things as they are'—lacking any inherent existence at their core but fully vibrant in their manifestation." Buddhism and quantum physics share certain ideas about reality, Mu Soeng suggests. "In the world of subatomic particles, there are no objects, only processes." Similarly, the Perfection of Wisdom teaching holds that what we perceive as objects are processes—causes and conditions arising in dynamic relationship. "Thus a more appropriate and accessible way to understand shunyata may be to understand it as 'momentariness' or 'transitoriness' rather than 'emptiness,'" he says.

Two Truths

Closely related to shunyata is the Madhyamaka teaching of two truths—relative and ultimate. Relative or conventional truth refers to samsara, the everyday, dualistic world of appearances. Absolute or ultimate truth is the true nature of reality: emptiness, which is non-dual. In a relative sense—in the ordinary world—things certainly exist. The car you drive to work, the bow you tie in your daughter's hair, the tears you cry when someone you love is in pain: these are not hallucinations. But they are what Mu Soeng calls "momentary manifestations in time and space; while the form lasts it has validity. But this appearance is transitory," he points out.

Relative and absolute truth are not separate; they are just two different views of essential oneness. A Zen saying expresses the paradox: "Things are not as they seem, nor are they otherwise."

Buddha Nature

While for Theravada Buddhists the path to enlightenment involves developing the qualities of a Buddha, the Mahayana view is that all sentient beings have the potential to attain enlightenment and realize their true nature. A central doctrine of the Yogacara school, Buddha Nature is not a quality—not something we have—but something we are. It is the intrinsic nature of a Buddha, which is emptiness.

Buddha Nature is always present but can be obscured by defilements and negative mind states. Through practice, we can clear the defilements and uncover our true nature.

The Mahayana Mahaparinirvana Sutra (Nirvana Sutra), one of several to put forth the teaching on Buddha Nature, was translated into Chinese from Sanskrit in the fifth century CE and became central to Chan/Zen Buddhism. In the famous Zen koan "Show me your original face, the face you had before your parents were born," original face refers to Buddha Nature.

Renunciation

Renunciation is a core teaching of Buddhist monasticism. In Theravada Buddhism, known as the path of renunciation, abstaining from practices that interfere with the goal of liberation is primary. In Mahayana Buddhism, renunciation has a slightly different meaning. Letting go of attitudes and patterns that hinder awakening is still important, but on the bodhisattva path, the quest for enlightenment is motivated by a compassionate desire to awaken for the benefit of all beings. Renunciation is said to help in developing bodhicitta.

Renunciation is a tricky concept for modern Westerners, who tend to associate it with Christian hairshirt penance or the extreme austerities of the Buddha's early quest for enlightenment. For Buddhist practitioners today, however, renunciation is less about externals—giving up worldly goods and sensory pleasure—than about relinquishing attachments to them and finding balance in one's life. In a *Lion's Roar* forum, Elizabeth Mattis-Namgyel, a Western Tibetan Buddhist teacher and author whose teacher, Dzigar Kongtrul Rinpoche, is also her husband, said that he "often uses the phrase 'little needs, much contentment.' If we have few needs and much contentment, we experience the wealth of the world around us, and when we experience that wealth there's nothing we need to renounce and nothing we need to add to it."

Refuge

Making a vow to adhere to the five lay precepts is one of the first steps to making a formal commitment to follow a Buddhist path. The other is taking refuge, also referred to as going for refuge. Taking refuge is a threefold vow to uphold the Triple Gem or Three Jewels—the Buddha, Dharma, and Sangha—and lead a life based on Buddhist principles. Broadly speaking, as Zen Master Robert Aitken Roshi suggests in *The Mind of Clover*, "Buddha, Dharma, and Sangha can be understood here to mean realization, truth, and harmony."

Although the Refuge Vow is an inner one, it is often repeated aloud in some sort of formal ceremony led by a Buddhist lama or monk. In the Tibetan Buddhist tradition, taking refuge is among the preliminary practices known as **ngondro,** (pronounced NOON dro) that prepare the student for deeper teachings and practices.

The vow itself is stated simply, here in Pali and English.

Buddham Saranam Gacchami
I take refuge in the Buddha. (If you prefer, you can use the
    phrase *I go for refuge . . .*)

Dhammam Saranam Gacchami
I take refuge in the Dharma.

Sangham Saranam Gacchami
I take refuge in the Sangha.

The vow is repeated three times. In many Buddhist temples or meditation centers, saying the Refuge Vow is part of a daily service. Some individuals include the vow in a personal daily practice ritual, repeating it before a home altar on which a Buddha image is displayed. Out of respect, they might also light a candle and incense and make an offering of flowers.

The simplicity of the refuge vow belies its significance in supporting and protecting the practitioner on the path of liberation. As Insight meditation teacher Gil Fronsdal explains it in his essay "Going for Refuge," *sarana*—Pali for refuge—means both a place to find safety and a sanctuary to protect something valuable. Taking the refuge vow encompasses both of those meanings.

On an external level, refuge in the Buddha is a commitment to accepting him as our model of awakening: his example shows us what we can attain in the pursuit of truth. This is "not taking refuge in him as a person," Bhikkhu Bodhi explains in *Going for Refuge & Taking the Precepts*, "but taking refuge in the fact of his Awakening: placing trust in the belief that he did awaken to the truth, that he did so by developing qualities we too can develop, and that the truths to which he awoke provide the best perspective for the conduct of our life."

Refuge in the Dharma means accepting the Buddha's teachings, his path of practice as our guide to attaining enlightenment. Taking refuge in the Sangha means making a commitment to the Buddha's followers, to the community of supportive spiritual companions.

The internal refuge consists of "inner states and capacities that we all have," Fronsdal points out. Drawing on these is what the Buddha meant by, "Be your own refuge. Take the Dharma as your refuge." Inner refuge in the Buddha gives us "confidence in our potential for spiritual growth," Fronsdal suggests, while taking inner refuge in the Dharma is a dedication to non-harming. Inner refuge in the Sangha supports our natural capacity for goodness in our relations with others.

If taking refuge means protection from danger, what, exactly, do we need protection from? Refuge can't protect us from adversity we encounter in life: "It can only safeguard us from the dangers of a negative response—from anxiety, sorrow, frustration, and despair." Bhikkhu Bodhi says. "Since we cannot alter the nature of the world to make it harmonize with our will, the only alternative is to change ourselves, by putting away attachment and aversion towards the world. We have to relinquish our clinging, to stop hankering and grasping, to learn to view the fluctuation of events with a detached equanimity free from the swing of elation and dejection."

Taking refuge aligns us with the power of the Buddhist path of practice to release us from attachment, aversion, and ignorance. In the Buddha's day, just one encounter with the Buddha was often enough for many to take refuge. As Karen Armstrong, a noted religion author, writes in *Buddha,* "He was a haven of peace in a violent world of clamorous egotism."

In our "violent world of clamorous egotism" today, 2,600 years later, the Buddha inspires similar feelings. He stands as a vivid reminder that awakening from delusion and self-centered fear is truly possible and that we too can embody compassion as a way of life.

THE THIRD TURNING OF THE WHEEL
OF DHARMA: VAJRAYANA

The Third Turning of the Wheel of Dharma initially referred to the central teachings of the Yogacara school of Mahayana Buddhism. Later, as Tibetan Buddhism rose to prominence, the Tibetans began using the Third Turning designation to refer to Vajrayana.

Vajrayana, or Tibetan Buddhism, is Mahayana Buddhism ratcheted up a few notches, with elaborate rituals and practices, secret teachings, gurus, and empowerments—initiations—deployed in the service of transformation. *Vajra,* literally "thunderbolt," by extension means diamond and indestructible weapon; since **yana** means "vehicle," Vajrayana is the Diamond Vehicle, which cuts through delusion rapidly and with precision. The Theravada and Mahayana traditions are said to be gradual paths, with enlightenment achieved over lifetimes. Vajrayana is said to be the fast track, with awakening achievable in a single lifetime. Theravada is known as the path of renunciation, Mahayana the path of the bodhisattva, and Vajrayana the path of transformation.

Vajrayana shares with Theravada and Mahayana basic teachings including the Four Noble Truths, the Eightfold Path, karma, dependent origination, and rebirth, and practices like taking refuge, renunciation, and meditation. With Mahayana Buddhism, it shares teachings on wisdom and compassion, Buddha nature, and emptiness. But while the Theravada and Mahayana traditions are grounded in teachings of the sutras, Vajrayana is rooted in esoteric Indian teachings known as **tantras.**

The further Buddhism gets from the historical Buddha, the more complex the teachings and practices become. The transformation practices that tantra introduced into Vajrayana aim toward realization of one's Buddha nature and involve visualizations, *mantras* (chants using sacred syllables), *mudras* (ritual hand gestures), *mandalas* (sacred circular diagrams representing divine realms, used in meditation), and various ritual objects. Ritual in Tibetan Buddhism practice is more intricate than in other Buddhist traditions. Temples and meditation halls are generally colorful and ornate, filled with sacred art and objects. Teachings, ceremonies, and empowerments (initiations into certain practices) may involve multiple lamas and attendants, monks and nuns, chanting, music with ritual instruments, sacred dances, recitation of texts, repetition of vows, and ritual feasts known as *ganachakras*.

Preliminaries

The Vajrayana path traditionally begins with *ngondro,* preliminary or foundational practices intended to prepare the mind for the higher practices to come. According to Thubten Chodron, an American Tibetan Buddhist nun who founded Sravasti Abbey in Newport, Washington, the process involves clearing karmic residue of past actions, as well as distractions that might hinder concentration. "On a psychological level, the preliminary practices alleviate much of the guilt and uncomfortable feelings we have been carrying around for years," she explains in an introduction to practices for clearing the mind, published on her website.

The preliminary practices include contemplation of the four thoughts that turn the mind to enlightenment—precious human birth; death and impermanence; karma; and the suffering of samsara—along with prostrations, taking refuge, arousing bodhicitta, mandala offerings, purification, and reciting mantras. Practices like mantras and prostrations are generally repeated one hundred thousand times.

An important part of ngondro is *guru yoga*—establishing the relationship with one's **guru**, the lama or teacher. From the beginning, the guru's role is critical. The guru guides the student along the path, conducting the ceremonies initiating the student into the practices and giving instructions in meditation and techniques for removing obstacles encountered in practice. In Vajrayana, the teachings are one-to-one, transmitted directly from guru to student with no intermediary; a close bond between the two is paramount. This is a devotional path: the student sees the guru as the Buddha; the guru serves as a role model for the student and offers unconditional love. This energetic exchange is so powerful that it can trigger awakening.

In the initiation ceremony, the guru plants a "seed" of enlightenment in the mind of the student that through practice ripens. Empowerment authorizes the student to perform the various stages of practice associated with a particular deity used as a meditation object. The empowerment ritual is intended "to engender faith in the disciples," Bruce Newman writes in *A Beginner's Guide to Tibetan Buddhism*. "They should feel committed to what lies ahead."

Deity Yoga

Preliminaries completed, the student generally begins deity practice under the guidance of the guru. Through meditation and rituals, the practitioner identifies with a *yidam,* a deity or Buddha-figure, as a vehicle of transformation. The creation or generation stage involves visualizing the yidam with any associated deities in a *mandala,* a symbolic picture of a "divine realm"—the deity's palace and its environment—and then identifying with the deity. In the completion or perfection stage the visualization is dissolved into emptiness. Yidams associated with outer tantras are peaceful deities, such as Manjushri, the bodhisattva of wisdom, and Tara, a bodhisattva said to be born from Avalokiteshvara's eye. In her manifestation as White Tara, she embodies compassion and is known as the "Mother of all Buddhas," said to grant happiness and long life. Inner tantras involve wrathful deities or deities in symbolic union.

Tantric practice involves working with powerful subtle energies. Depending on the tradition, there are four or six classes of tantras, which are distinguished by, the teacher Alexander Berzin explains, "an increasing level of bliss awareness used to focus on voidness (emptiness)." The highest, or most advanced, tantra involves visualization of symbolic union between a deity and consort. Many tantric practices are secret teachings, both to protect the integrity and sacredness of the teachings and to prevent them from being misunderstood by, or even harmful to, the uninitiated.

Much is made of Buddhism being a non-theistic religion, so it may be confusing to encounter the prevalence of deity-centered rituals and practices. Unlike the gods and goddesses of mythology and certain spiritual traditions, the deities used in tantric practice are not objects of supplication for help with lost causes or lost car keys. They are embodiments or expressions of essential qualities latent within us, intended to guide us in manifesting our true nature.

In the Theravada tradition, practice aims at transcending or purifying negative mind states. In Mahayana Buddhism, known as the causal vehicle, practice is the cause or means to produce the fruit of the path: discovering one's inherent Buddha nature. Vajrayana is known as the resultant or fruition vehicle: practice is based on uncovering the fruit, the Buddha that we already are.

Vajrayana works with emotions and mind states just as they are, in all their disarray. "Tantrism uses emotional conflicts as well as concepts in order to go beyond delusion," Traleg Kyabgon Rinpoche explains in *The Essence of Buddhism*. "The way the concepts are used is through the practice of visualization, and as one becomes more acquainted with the visualizations they become more and more complex and demanding. Instead of abandoning concepts, however, one uses them. At the same time, one uses the conflicting emotions in order to transform them into their corresponding wisdoms."

Dzogchen

Many Buddhist practitioners today are drawn to dzogchen. Known as the Great Perfection, meaning "accomplishment or fulfillment that is complete," dzogchen is the path of self-liberation. It is practiced in all four of the main Tibetan Buddhist traditions, but is most closely associated with the Nyingma tradition and with Bön, the indigenous religion of Tibet.

The ground or base of dzogchen is the primordially pure, non-dual essence of the natural mind. The essence is emptiness:

images, thoughts, sensations arise in and leave the natural mind without changing its pure state, just as clouds arise and disappear without changing the fundamental nature of the sky. Dzogchen practice is direct realization of this natural state through contemplation of body, speech, and mind. Unlike the sutra traditions, dzogchen does not involve getting rid of, perfecting, or transforming any experience of body, speech, or mind. Whatever arises is allowed to just be. Then, working on the physical, mental, and energetic levels, the practitioner draws attention to negative emotions and painful blocks, and without trying to change them, simply sits with them until the afflictions dissolve naturally—until they self-liberate.

4

⟨⟩

THE PRACTICES

From accounts of the Buddha's teachings, it sometimes seems as if all his listeners had to do was hear him speak once and they were immediately enlightened. Spontaneous awakening does happen for some people, but for most the path to enlightenment is gradual. The mind "ripens" slowly with continual practice over time, until at some point it opens. Awakening might feel sudden then because there is a noticeable shift in perception. But it has been preceded by a lot of dedicated preparation.

The Buddha was pretty clear how the process works. In a teaching at what is now the holy city of Varanasi he said:

The attainment of [wisdom] is after gradual training, gradual action, gradual practice . . . Having heard the Dhamma, one remembers it. Remembering, one penetrates the meaning of the teachings. Penetrating the meaning . . . desire [for awakening] arises. When desire has arisen, one is willing. When one is

*willing, one contemplates. Having contemplated, one makes an
exertion. Having made an exertion, one realizes with the body the
ultimate truth, and having penetrated it with discernment, sees it.*

The last section of the Eightfold Path is Concentration,
which contains Right Effort, Right Mindfulness, and Right
Concentration. For most Westerners, interest in Buddhism begins here, with meditation practice. For many, meditation remains their primary connection to the Dharma.

The Buddha, however, said that in order to reap the most
benefit from practice, we have to prepare the ground. The first
preliminary he suggested is generosity. Certainly generosity is
an important quality, but you might wonder how it's con-
nected to meditation. Thanissaro Bhikkhu—an American, born
Geoffrey DeGraff, who trained in the Thai Forest tradition in
Asia and is now abbot of Metta Forest Monastery near San
Diego, California—says that cultivating generosity helps us
"begin the long process of weakening the unawakened practitioner's habitual tendencies to cling—to views, to sensuality,
to unskillful modes of thought and behavior." In that way, it
functions much like ngondro practices in Vajrayana.

Practicing the Five Lay Precepts is recommended next. That
provides, Thanissaro Bhikkhu says, "the basic level of sense-
restraint that helps the practitioner develop a healthy and
trustworthy sense of self." The rest of the Buddha's gradual
training includes renunciation and a deep dive into the Four
Noble Truths before we finally get to our meditation cushions. The point of all that isn't to make us crazy, but to prepare us for the ultimate happiness—awakening.

The Buddha's early followers were single-mindedly pursuing

enlightenment. Maybe you are too. On the other hand, perhaps all this is new to you and you would just like to dip your
toe in the water and try meditation practice. That's a fine
place to start. "Just as we might practice the piano to cultivate
our musical ability or practice a sport to cultivate our athletic
ability, we can practice meditation to nurture the natural
ability of the mind to be present, to feel loving-kindness, to
open beyond fixed opinions and views," Pema Chödrön
writes in *Living Beautifully with Uncertainty and Change*. Meditation is beneficial on many levels. Jay Michaelson, a political
columnist and meditation teacher, touts its stress-relieving
value: "Creating islands of calm amid the insanity of our culture enables me to rest, recharge, and go back to the work of
justice."

Cultivating the Mind of Enlightenment

Buddhist meditation plays a vital role on the path to inner freedom. In *What the Buddha Taught*, Walpola Rahula explains that
practice "aims at cleansing the mind of impurities and distur-
bances such as lustful desires, hatred, ill-will, indolence, worries
and restlessness, skeptical doubts, and cultivating such qualities
as concentration, awareness, intelligence, will, energy, the analytical faculty, joy, tranquility, finally leading to the attainment
of highest wisdom which sees the nature of things as they are
and realizes the Ultimate Truth, Nirvana."

Right Effort, the first of the three factors in the Concentration section of the Eightfold Path, means generating the desire
and persistence to let go of negative attitudes that interfere with
concentration and cultivate beneficial qualities that support it.

Meditation is the appropriate vehicle for "producing a state of perfect health, equilibrium, and tranquility," Rahula asserts, but we have to focus our energy in the right direction to reap the benefits.

Preparing to Sit

You've done the preparations. You're ready to meditate. Now there's a practical consideration: how to sit. It might seem as if it's okay just to plop down anywhere, but finding a way to sit that is comfortable and supportive is essential for getting the most out of practice. Guidelines on posture vary by tradition; some contain five, six, or even nine points to consider. Whatever the number, these are the common elements:

• **Seat** A stable seat allows you to concentrate on your practice rather than on your aching knees. The traditional meditation posture is to sit on a cushion on the floor. Or you can kneel, supported by either cushions or a bench designed for meditation. If you are more comfortable in a chair, choose one with a flat seat, straight back, and no arms.

• **Legs** If you are sitting on a cushion, cross your legs in front of you. There are several possible positions into which you can fold your legs: full lotus, half lotus, Burmese style, or the way you might cross your legs sitting around a campfire. If you are sitting on a chair, either keep your legs uncrossed with both feet flat on the floor or cross your legs at the ankle. (For photos of sitting postures, with detailed instructions, see www.insightmeditationcenter.org/books-articles/articles/postures-for-meditation/)

• **Back** "Sit light and easy," suggests Bhante Henepola Guna-ratana in his best-selling meditation manual, *Mindfulness in Plain English*. "The spine should be like a firm young tree growing out of soft ground. The rest of the body just hangs from it in a loose, relaxed manner." A straight back will help you concentrate and avoid drowsiness. Tuck your chin slightly to prevent a stiff neck. If you are sitting on a chair, try not to lean against the chair back.

• **Hands** Unless your meditation leader instructs you to use a particular mudra (hand position), you can rest your hands lightly in your lap with palms open, one hand cradled in the other with thumbs touching lightly. Or you can rest your hands on your thighs.

• **Eyes** Meditating with your eyes open helps you stay alert. With a soft focus, gaze slightly downward at a spot a few feet in front of you. If you concentrate better with closed eyes, open them if you start to nod off.

• **Mouth** Relax your jaw, allowing your mouth to soften. You can rest your tongue lightly against the roof of your mouth.

How Long to Practice

Wondering how long to meditate? The Vietnamese Zen master Thich Nhat Hanh suggests starting with twenty or thirty minutes. "After about fifteen minutes or so, it is possible to reach a deep quiet filled with inner peace and joy," he writes in *The Miracle of Mindfulness*. If twenty minutes feels too long at first, you could begin with five or ten minutes, then increase the time in five-minute increments until you are able to sit for half an hour or longer. As your meditation time increases, your ability to concentrate will improve and you will feel your practice deepen.

Practicing the Buddhist Way

Right Concentration and Right Mindfulness are the points on the Noble Eightfold Path that specifically relate to meditation. Each describes a different mental faculty. Right Concentration *(samadhi)* refers to one-pointed focus. Right Mindfulness *(sati)* refers to insight.

The Buddha taught mindfulness as the way to end suffering. These days the term is used in many different ways. As Joseph Goldstein defines it in *One Dharma*, "Mindfulness, the method, is the key to the present. Without it, we simply stay lost in the wanderings of our mind." Broadly speaking, mindfulness isn't a single practice but a state of wakeful awareness that can be developed through practice. To Jon Kabat-Zinn, who has long taught meditation as the key to maintaining compassion and sanity amid the "full catastrophe" of daily life, "Mindfulness means paying attention in a particular way: on purpose, in the present moment, and non-judgmentally."

Sometimes mindfulness is used interchangeably with insight, as in insight meditation—another name for Vipassana. Concentration and mindfulness often work together. In *Mindfulness in Plain English*, Bhante G., as his followers call him, defines concentration as the "faculty of the mind that focuses single-pointedly on one object without interruption" and mindfulness as "a delicate function leading to refined sensibilities." In practice, they are complementary:

Mindfulness is the sensitive one. It notices things. Concentration provides the power. It keeps the attention pinned down to one item . . . Mindfulness picks the objects of attention, and notices when the attention has gone astray. Concentration does the actual work of holding the attention steady on that chosen object.

SHAMATHA

Shamatha, or "calm abiding," is a basic practice in every Buddhist tradition. Its aim is to develop one-pointed concentration. It cultivates what Bhante G., in *The Jhanas in Theravada Buddhist Meditation*, calls "a calm, concentrated, unified mind as a means of experiencing inner peace and as a basis for wisdom."

There are many possible objects of focus for shamatha practice: a mantra or sacred syllable, a Zen koan, a *mala* (meditation beads used to count breaths or mantra repetitions), a visualization, a mandala or some other sacred image. The simplest and most commonly used object is the breath.

Sometimes people confuse shamatha with samadhi. Shamatha is a practice for achieving concentration, while **samadhi** refers to a deeply concentrated state in which the mind is stilled. (See **Jhanas, or Meditative Absorptions**, page 131.)

Practice: *In-and-Out Breath Meditation*

Mindfulness of breathing—observing the breath—is a form of meditation known as *Anapanasati* in Pali. (*Sati* means "mindfulness"; *anapana* refers to breathing in and out. Often referred to simply as Anapana, this is a core form of meditation as well as a first step in Vipassana practice.

At the nose: Place your attention at your nostrils, or just below your nose in the space between the nostrils and your upper lip. As you inhale and exhale, be aware of each breath. Breathe naturally, without forcing the breath or changing the tempo. As thoughts arise, don't follow them or try to suppress them. Just gently guide your attention back to the breath.

Focusing the breath at the nostrils was favored by the renowned meditation master S. N. Goenka, who introduced thousands of Westerners to Vipassana. Of Indian heritage but born and raised in Burma, Goenka left a successful business career to teach a non-sectarian approach to traditional Burmese practices. (For a ten-minute meditation guided by Goenka, go to Vipassana Org's YouTube channel at www.youtube.com /watch?v=Oh5ii6R6LTM.)

At the abdomen: If you prefer, you can follow the in-and-out movement of the breath at your abdomen. Some people find that placing their hands lightly on the abdomen as they breathe helps them to keep their attention focused there.

Observing the breath at the abdomen was the preferred technique of another great Burmese teacher, the Theravada Buddhist monk Mahasi U Sobhana Sayadaw. (Sayadaw—Burmese for "royal teacher"—is an honorific for a senior monk.) Following the rising and falling of the breath at the abdomen rather than at the nostrils allows the meditator to sustain closer contact with the body, the Sayadaw taught. (For Mahasi Sayadaw's instructions in Vipassana, see page 128.)

Practice: *Counting Breaths*

For a stronger support for concentration, you can count breaths. This method is often used by beginners in zazen (Zen meditation). Breathe naturally, counting each exhalation from one to ten. After the tenth exhalation, start again at one. If your mind wanders and you lose count, don't worry, it happens to us all. Just gently return your attention to the breath and begin counting again at one. When a thought arises, don't follow it or try to get rid of it. Just return to counting.

VIPASSANA, INSIGHT MEDITATION

Vipassana, or Insight meditation, comes under the heading of Right Meditation on the Eightfold Path. It offers "insight into the nature of things, leading to the complete liberation of mind," Walpola Rahula states in *What the Buddha Taught*. "It is an analytical method based on mindfulness, awareness, vigilance, observation."

The Buddha's central teaching on insight practice is the Satipatthana Sutta, the Foundations of Mindfulness. Rahula calls it "the most important discourse ever given by the Buddha on mental development." It is so venerated, he says, that Theravada Buddhist families in Asia gather in their homes and read the text aloud. Not likely to happen in a Western home, but it suggests how central mindfulness teachings are to Buddhist practice.

Mahasi Sayadaw, who died in 1982, was among the meditation teachers Joseph Goldstein studied with in Asia. The Sayadaw is known by meditators the world over for his method of insight practice. It is the primary approach to Vipassana taught in America today.

Grounded in the Buddha's Four Foundations of Mindfulness, Mahasi Sayadaw's technique is a particular form of close observation he called "noting." The breath, body sensations, thoughts, and movements are marked with a mental note. A breath is noted as "rising, falling," a thought as "thinking, thinking." Even the imaginary conversations in your head are noted as "speaking, speaking." When nearly every physical and mental activity is observed and noted, the mind is less likely to wander into samsaric byways. But the Sayadaw acknowledged its natural propensity to wander off to faraway places. And when it strays, "the wandering mind should not be let alone," his instructions indicate in *Satipatthana Vipassana*. "It should be noted as 'wandering, wandering.'"

Contemplation in this manner is so thorough, so deep that it leads not only to improved concentration but also to insight into the truth of suffering, impermanence, and non-self, the Sayadaw says in *Thoughts on the Dhamma*, selections from his talks. "Insight knowledge is obtained by observing the actions of mind-and-body in the state of impermanence, suffering, and no-self. It is not attained simply by casual observation but by in-depth observation of actions as they are happening."

Mahasi Sayadaw could not overstress the importance of direct experience—awareness of what is happening in the moment, without judgment or commentary. "Watch a flash of lightning," he enjoins in *A Discourse on* To Nibbana via the Noble Eightfold Path. "If you are imagining in your mind as to how lightning strikes before or after the event, you may not be regarded as having seen the flash of lightning. So try to know things for yourself by actual observation of things as they happen."

The instructions for noting are precise. The mental note should not be vocalized: "In vipassana meditation it is more important to know the object than to know it as a term or name," the Sayadaw explains in *Satipatthana Vipassana*. Similarly, no first-person pronoun is used in a note. It is not the self being observed, he says, but the senses and sense-contact—the seeing, not who sees. Actions should be carried out slowly, with each action duly noted. Noting should be continuous, with no break between one note and the next.

Practice: Noting

For a taste of what noting is like, try it for fifteen to twenty minutes or so, and then imagine a whole day spent that attentively. Pick an activity you normally do, such as getting dressed in the morning or preparing a meal. Then follow the Sayadaw's instructions and note every thought, action, and sensation as you become aware of it. If you prefer, you can do the noting exercise while walking (page 145).

As a sample of what the experience of noting is like, imagine you are in my seat as I practiced noting at dinner the other night. Total elapsed time for this exercise was about thirty-five seconds.

> *You are already seated. Begin noting by looking at the plate on the table before you and silently repeating, "looking, seeing, looking, seeing." You reach for a fork: "reaching, reaching." You pick up the fork: "touching, lifting, touching, lifting." You spear food with the fork: "gathering, gathering." You raise the fork to your mouth: "lifting, lifting." You open your mouth: "opening, opening." You take a bite: "placing, placing." You remove the fork from your mouth: "withdrawing, withdrawing." You return the fork to the plate: "lowering, placing, lowering, placing." You chew the food: "chewing, chewing." You taste the food: "tasting, tasting."*

You enjoy the food: "liking, liking." You swallow it: "swallowing, swallowing."

All that activity for one bite of dinner. But what a bite! Concentrating in that way, you can follow every physical and mental process of your experience, as you experience it. With practice, you may also begin to note other processes going on at the same time, such as breathing, body temperature, the feeling of air currents against the skin.

Jhanas, or Meditative Absorptions

Meditation absorptions called the *jhanas* are powerful ways to practice Right Concentration. In an interview by Mary Talbot for *Tricycle: The Buddhist Review*, Leigh Brasington, one of the few people teaching this practice in North America, defines the jhanas as "eight altered states of consciousness, each one requiring more concentration than the previous and each one generating more concentration than the previous." Passing through progressively higher mind states in the first four jhanas, the meditator experiences bliss, serenity, and equanimity. The last four, or "formless" jhanas, purify and concentrate the mind to attain enlightenment.

The Buddha practiced the jhanas with his two teachers in the forest before his enlightenment, reaching the highest level—"beyond perception and non-perception"—and he practiced them on the night of his enlightenment. It was remembering his spontaneous experience of the first jhana in childhood that inspired the Buddha to find the Middle Way between self-denial and self-indulgence. "Throughout his active career the four jhanas remained his heavenly dwelling to which he resorted to live happily here and now," Bhante Gunaratana notes in *The Jhanas in Theravada Buddhist Meditation.*

The first four of the eight jhanas are classic concentration practices. The first jhana is entered by generating what is called "access concentration." To get a taste of jhana practice, you can try the method here to raise access concentration and reach the first jhana. The practice is based on Leigh Brasington's instructions. Your meditation object is the breath.

PRACTICE: Entering the First Jhana

Before beginning, find a comfortable upright position you can remain in without moving for the duration of the meditation.

- Begin by placing your attention on the object of meditation, in this case your breath, and keeping it there. Continue to pay close attention to the breath.
- When your thoughts lessen and you are no longer distracted by them, you have reached access concentration. At this point, you are fully present with the breath. Your mind is free of anger, worry, or extraneous thoughts.
- Your breathing becomes shallower. If the breath becomes very subtle or seems to disappear, do *not* take a deep breath. Instead, shift your attention from the breath to a pleasant sensation in your body. It might be in the hands, at the heart, on the top of the head, at the third eye—the chakra or energy center located in the forehead between the eyebrows.

- Keep your attention on the pleasant sensation. Become immersed in it. Cultivate a calm and quiet mind focused on pleasantness.
- Then just let go. The jhana will arise on its own.
- The pleasant sensation will increase in intensity until you realize that you are in an altered mind state. A feeling of rapture (*piti*) will course through your body and mind, accompanied by a sense of happiness and joy (*sukkha*). You have now reached the first jhana.

The Brahma Viharas

Meditation on any of the four boundless states known as the Brahma Viharas, or Four Immeasurables is a beautiful way to generate positive regard for others and dissolve any sense of separation between ourselves and the world. Metta, or loving-kindness meditation, is the most familiar of the brahma vihara practices, but the practices of compassion, sympathetic joy, and equanimity are also very powerful. (For a fuller description of the Brahma Viharas, see page 96.)

PRACTICE: Metta, or Loving-kindness

Loving-kindness, or metta, is unconditional love for all beings, with a wholehearted wish for them to be happy. Loving-kindness practice is based on warmth without self-interest.

In this meditation, we generate loving-kindness and a genuine wish for all beings to be happy, healthy, safe, and live with ease. The practice counteracts greed or aversion that obscures our natural friendliness. We begin by directing loving-kindness toward ourselves and then gradually widen our circle of caring until we are sending unconditional love to all beings everywhere. Some people may find it difficult at first to send lovingkindness to themselves, notes Sharon Salzberg. But this is an essential step in the process and must not be omitted, she emphasizes.

As a formal practice, "we gently repeat phrases that are meaningful in terms of what we wish, first for ourselves and then for others," Salzberg suggests in *Lovingkindness*. We can either create phrases of our own, she says, or use traditional ones.

> *May I be happy.*
> *May I be healthy.*
> *May I be safe.*
> *May I live with ease.*

When sending metta to others, use the second-person pronoun (*May you be happy*).

Sit comfortably. Close your eyes or not. Take a few deep breaths, then let the breath settle. Begin by generating lovingkindness for yourself, silently repeating each phase slowly: *May I be happy. May I be healthy. May I be safe. May I live with ease.* The aspiration *May I live with ease* "is not a wish for luxury," Salzberg points out in *Love Your Enemies,* "but rather that your livelihood and relationships and other aspects of daily life not be a struggle."

After you have repeated the phrases for yourself for a few minutes, think of someone you consider a benefactor: someone who has inspired or helped you or been kind or generous in some way—a teacher or mentor, perhaps. Bring your benefactor to mind and offer the phrases to that person.

Next, think of a dear friend or family member whose life is going pretty well at the moment. See that person in your mind's eye and offer the phrases of loving-kindness. Or think of a dear friend or family member who is not doing so well, one who is ill, perhaps, or having a difficult time. Bring that friend to mind and offer the phrases of loving-kindness.

Next, think of a person you have neutral feelings toward. Perhaps it is someone you see in your daily life but don't really know—the checkout clerk at the supermarket, the bus driver on your commute, the barista who makes your espresso latte. Offer that person the phrases.

Now think of a difficult person—someone you feel resentment toward, someone who has hurt you, perhaps. Bring that person to mind and offer them loving-kindness. Sharon Salzberg suggests waiting until you have done this practice for a while before offering loving-kindness to an enemy or other really challenging person.

Finally, offer loving-kindness to all beings everywhere.

Loving-kindness meditation opens your heart to others. Even difficult people begin to seem less threatening. Practitioners report miraculous turnarounds in which enemies have become dear friends. Your outpouring of warm feeling is healing to all concerned—yourself included. And you don't have to wait until you are sitting in formal meditation to practice loving-kindness, Sharon Salzberg points out in *Love Your Enemies*. "It is a practice you can ultimately take with you anywhere—walking down the street, sitting on the bus, waiting for a doctor's appointment." (A good place to do it is while you're in the dentist's chair. Sending the dentist loving-kindness helps to ease your pain—psychologically, at least.)

PRACTICE: Compassion

Compassion, or karuna, the second Brahma Vihara, is the wish for all beings to be free of suffering. "Practicing compassion counteracts cruelty," Salzberg says in *Love Your Enemies*. It strengthens our ability to identify with others, allowing us to confront their pain without shrinking from it or feeling overwhelmed by it. By remaining fully present in the face of suffering we can offer emotional support and provide substantive help where needed.

Compassion practice is similar to loving-kindness practice but uses a different sequence and different phrases. You start not with yourself but with someone you know who is really suffering. Be specific, Sharon Salzberg emphasizes. The intention at this point is to arouse compassion for an individual, not for a category of sufferers, such as homeless people or refugees. You can create a phrase or phrases specific to the situation, or use a more general phrase like *May you be happy and free of suffering,* or *May you be healthy and pain-free.*

After you have directed compassion to the person for a few minutes, you can stop, or you can move through the rest of the loving-kindness sequence, repeating the phrases. (Now's the time to broaden your caring to those refugees, if you wish.)

PRACTICE: Sympathetic Joy

The third Brahma Vihara, sympathetic joy, or mudita, is delight in others' happiness and good fortune. Sympathetic joy is an antidote to jealousy and resentment. The practice of arousing it helps us overcome feelings of deprivation and envy.

For this practice, you might use a phrase like *May your happiness and good fortune increase* or *May your success be undiminished* or *May your happiness be unbounded.* Even better is to take the opportunity to think up a phrase that specifically fits the person and the occasion. Start by focusing on someone dear to you who is enjoying some success or happiness at the moment. Skip yourself, as the whole point of the practice is to rejoice for someone else. To counter any feelings of lack, Sharon Salzberg suggests ending the practice by reflecting on what you can be grateful for in your own life.

PRACTICE: Equanimity

Equanimity, upekkha, is inner balance—what Salzberg calls "the unspoken wisdom that allows us to broaden our caring beyond our own inner circle, making the practices of loving-kindness, compassion, and sympathetic joy true expressions of a generous spirit."

Equanimity comes from accepting the reality of life's ups and downs—the eight vicissitudes or worldly conditions (page 90). Salzberg suggests beginning equanimity practice with a neutral person, moving on to a benefactor, and then progressing through the rest of the sequence, ending with yourself. You can compose your own phrase or you can use one of Salzberg's phrases, such as *May all beings find peace* or *May we all accept things as they are.*

Tonglen

Tonglen, Tibetan for "taking and sending," is a Tibetan Buddhist practice that allows us to take the suffering of another and exchange it for our happiness and well-being. Instead of obsessing over our own suffering, we can express love and compassion for another being who is in pain. (Yes, that includes a pet as well.) Tonglen is a win-win, points out Tibetan Buddhist monk Matthieu Ricard in *Altruism: The Power of Compassion to Change Yourself and the World.* "Altruistic love and compassion are the most powerful antidotes to our own torments."

PRACTICE: Tonglen

To begin, bring to mind someone you care about who is suffering in some way. Visualize that person. Feel your love and concern for the person. Empathize with whatever physical or emotional pain they are experiencing. Then take a deep breath and as you inhale, imagine that you are breathing in that person's suffering, that you are taking in all their anguish, all their difficulties. Visualize that pain as thick, dark smoke. As you breathe, feel the pain transform into joy and visualize the dark smoke dissipating, leaving clean, clear air. Exhale, sending the person the clear air, along with your joy, love, and happiness, and a feeling of well-being.

PRACTICE: Tonglen for All Beings

Matthieu Ricard offers a variation on the basic tonglen practice to transform the suffering of all beings everywhere. Imagine beings all over the world. Then inhale as before, taking in their suffering as a dense, black cloud. Allow the cloud to penetrate your heart, where it dissolves into white light. As you exhale, imagine "that your heart is a brilliant sphere of light from which rays of white light carry your happiness to all beings, all over the world."

PRACTICE: Tonglen for the Universe

If you are feeling particularly expansive, you might try another variation from Matthieu Ricard. "Imagine that you multiply into an infinity of forms that reach far out into the universe." Take on the suffering of all beings you encounter, then offer them your happiness in whatever form they need, so that "you become clothing for people who are cold, food for the hungry, or refuge for the homeless."

Mantra

Mantra practice is used in both the Mahayana and Vajrayana traditions. It involves repeating a sacred syllable, word, phrase, or sound as a meditative object to calm and concentrate the mind. The Sanskrit word *mantra* means "mind protector." In Vajrayana, a mantra is often used to prepare the mind to receive Buddhist teachings and the blessings and protection of specific deities.

The most familiar mantra in Buddhism is *Om mani padme hum,* which is associated with the bodhisattva of compassion, Avalokiteshvara—Chenrezig in Tibetan. Repeating this mantra invokes the blessing of Chenrezig and generates compassion in the practitioner. Throughout the Himalayan region the mantra is etched into rocks called *mani* stones, and written versions are sealed inside the tubular prayer wheels that are ubiquitous in the Tibetan world. It is said that spinning a prayer wheel containing the mantra has the same power to invoke the benevolence of Chenrezig as chanting the mantra silently or aloud.

While *Om mani padme hum* cannot be translated directly, it is usually said to mean "The jewel is in the lotus" or "Praise to the jewel in the lotus."

In a talk at the Kalmyk Mongolian Buddhist Center in New Jersey, the Dalai Lama explained the meaning of the syllables and the importance of this mantra. *Om* or *aum* symbolizes the impure body, speech, and mind of the practitioner and the pure body, speech, and mind of the Buddha into which the impure body is transformed. *Mani*, meaning "jewel," symbolizes the method by which transformation occurs: the bodhisattva path with the altruistic intention to become enlightened to help all sentient beings. *Padme*, "lotus," symbolizes wisdom. This is the wisdom that realizes impermanence, non-self, and emptiness—the oneness of existence. *Hum* symbolizes the indivisibility of wisdom and method (compassion) and is the seed syllable—a mantra condensed into one sound— associated with the wisdom Buddha, Akshobhya the Imperturbable.

Through the practice of *Om mani padme hum*—representing the indivisible union of wisdom and compassion—we realize the pure body, speech, and mind of the Buddha within.

The six syllables of the mantra are generally pronounced "ohm mah nee pahd may hoom" ("oo" sound as in *book*). Tibetans often chant the mantra using the syllables "ohm mah nee peh may hoong."

You will often see people chanting *Om mani padme hum* while fingering the beads of a mala—a Buddhist rosary—or spinning a Tibetan Buddhist prayer wheel.

Hindrances to Meditation

Just when your meditation practice is starting to cook, suddenly you hit a wall. Or maybe just a bump in the road. It happens to everyone. It's so common that the Buddhists have a name for the difficulties we may encounter: the five hindrances. Sensual desire; ill-will; sloth and torpor; restlessness and remorse; doubt—these are the classic obstacles or "overgrowths of the mind that stultify insight," as the Buddha called them. Mind states that work against concentration, they can block the path to awakening. Doubt is said to be the most serious of the hindrances, as it can lead us to give up practice.

There are a variety of ways to deal with these common obstacles. The Theravadan strategy is to investigate. Some years ago, mindfulness teacher Michelle McDonald came up with a practice that is now widely used for not only working with the five hindrances in formal practice but also dealing with the emotional challenges of everyday life. The practice goes by a handy acronym: RAIN.

R: Recognize
A: Accept
I: Investigate
N: Non-identification

A guide posted by the Insight Meditation Center suggests that "often just recognizing a hindrance is enough for it to fall away." If recognizing it and accepting it aren't enough, the next step is to investigate the hindrance "physically, emotionally, energetically, cognitively, and motivationally," followed by a practice to replace the negative emotion with a positive mind state. That might be metta practice to counter ill-will, for example, or contemplation of the body's deterioration or "unlovely parts" to quell sensual desire. Non-identification means seeing the hindrance as a passing event and not something that defines you.

"RAIN directly deconditions the habitual ways in which you resist your moment-to-moment experience," psychologist and meditation teacher Tara Brach explains in *True Refuge: Finding Peace and Freedom in Your Own Awakened Heart*. Founder of the Insight Meditation Community in Washington, DC, Brach has introduced thousands of meditators and mental health professionals to RAIN and has made it a core part of her own practice. "You can awaken recognition simply by asking yourself: 'What is happening inside me right now?'" Brach suggests. Then "with investigation you engage in a more active and pointed kind of inquiry." In going through the RAIN process, we may encounter some resistance, Brach acknowledges. It's only natural to resist uncomfortable feelings, but that's no reason to stop. "We need to offer a gentle welcome to whatever surfaces. This is why I use the phrase 'Investigate with kindness.'"

In the Mahayana approach, the practitioner might contemplate a hindrance to understand its impermanence and empty nature. With that realization, the pull of the hindrance disappears, and a positive mind state can arise in its place.

The Vajrayana approach to the hindrances might be *Bring it on!* "We do not reject anything; rather we make use of whatever is there," explains Ringu Tulku Rinpoche, a Tibetan Buddhist master in the Kagyu Order, in *Daring Steps: Traversing the Path of the Buddha.* "We look at our negative emotions and accept them for what they are. Then we relax in this state of acceptance. Using the emotion itself, it is transformed or transmuted into the positive, into its true face." When strong emotions are neither rejected nor followed, fascination with them disappears, and the hindrance no longer blocks concentration.

PRACTICE: Tilopa's Six Nails

Tilopa was an eleventh-to-twelfth century CE Indian *mahasiddha,* or great adept, who was famous for his pithy teachings. His Six Nails, or Six Words of Advice that "nail" his meaning—get it just right—are among his best-known instructions. Contemplation of these points is an effective way to deal with habitual patterns that hinder meditation.

The Tibetan text literally consists of just six words, but Ken McLeod, the Tibetan Buddhist teacher who translated the instructions into English, later fleshed out the advice in an extended translation that "some people prefer," McLeod says.

Don't recall.	Let go of what has passed.
Don't imagine.	Let go of what may come.
Don't think.	Let go of what is happening now.
Don't examine.	Don't try to figure anything out.
Don't control.	Don't try to make anything happen.
Rest.	Relax right now, and rest.

Despite their simplicity, Tilopa's nails go to the heart of the most common pitfalls we encounter in meditation practice. No matter how conscientious we are, the mind tends to wander off into ruminations about the past or concerns about the future. But when we stop dwelling on the past and the future, we can rest in the present moment. The instruction "Don't think" or "Let go of what is happening now" may seem contradictory. Isn't the point of meditation to be with what's happening now? So often, though, we are focusing on our internal dialogue about what's happening rather than directly experiencing the present moment. "Don't examine" exhorts us not to analyze our experience—*Am I doing it right? Am I enlightened yet?* "Don't control" and "Rest" are corollaries of that. Instead of trying to stage-manage every aspect of practice, Tilopa's advice is to release all expectations and demands, and rest in the moment. That leaves space for the fruit of our practice to ripen in its own time.

There are a number of ways to work with Tilopa's key points. Experiment to see what works best for you. One way would be to focus on an individual phrase as your meditation object. Another would be to bring to mind the appropriate point or points if your practice goes off track during meditation.

Mindful Walking

PRACTICE: Walking Just to Walk

Thich Nhat Hanh is known for the long, silent walks he leads, often trailing dozens of people behind him. Even a walk through the noise and hustle of New York City is a contemplative experience the way he does it. What makes this practice different from the way we usually walk is the intention. "Walking meditation is really to enjoy the walking—walking not in order to arrive, just for walking," he explains in *Present Moment, Wonderful Moment*. "The purpose is to be in the present moment and enjoy every step you make."

PRACTICE: Walking and Noting

Walking practice using the Vipassana method taught by the Burmese Theravada meditation master Mahasi Sayadaw involves silently noting each footstep. This is a very different walking experience from the way Zen master Thich Nhat Hanh does it.

Slow walking: This exercise should be done very slowly. Make sure to complete one step and place the foot on the ground before beginning to step with the other foot. To start, place your attention on your right foot and lift the foot slowly, noting "lifting, lifting." Move the foot forward slowly, noting "moving, moving." Place the foot on the ground, noting, "placing, placing." Repeat the same sequence with the left foot, then alternate feet, continuing to note. If you glance at your surroundings as you walk, note "looking, seeing."

Walking with normal or quick steps: For walking at a quicker pace, you can just note each full step as "left step, right step" or simply "walking, walking."

Living Mindfully

The Buddha constantly reminded his followers that his teachings were not theoretical; they were to be applied in every area of life. Thich Nhat Hanh is a master of extending mindfulness to everyday life and maintaining awareness in every moment. His many books contain dozens of simple instructions for consciously using everyday activities as practice—anything from taking out the garbage to getting dressed to half-smiling when irritated.

PRACTICE: Retreat Day

A growing number of Buddhist practitioners, along with others interested in mindfulness, are choosing to set aside one day a week or one day a month as a retreat day. For many, the retreat is a media fast, with cell phone, computer, and other digital gadgets turned off and tucked away out of sight. Part or all of the day might be devoted to meditation. It might be a day of silence and/or fasting. However it's spent, a retreat day can be transformative. When our habitual pace slows and the noise and distractions lessen, we can hear our thoughts and observe our habitual thinking. Life itself becomes a contemplative practice.

If you want to try a retreat day and you haven't done a retreat at home or at a retreat center, there are a few basics to consider in order to make the experience meaningful.

Intention: First, set an intention for your retreat. Maybe you want to start or deepen a meditation practice. Perhaps you have a decision to make or a problem you want to mull over. You may simply want some time for rest and relaxation. Having a focus for your retreat will help you in creating a schedule and deciding how you want to spend the time. If a full day of silence and solitude seems too daunting at first, you could start with a half-day retreat.

Setting: Choose a place where you will be undisturbed for the duration of the retreat. Nothing is harder than trying to achieve serenity amid a hive of activity and people making demands on your time. If you can't arrange to have your home to yourself or borrow a space from a friend, at least choose a quiet room. Be sure to let everyone know in advance that you will be on retreat and unavailable. If the weather is nice, consider spending some or all of your retreat outdoors. Nature is a great support for practice.

Create a dedicated meditation space. It can be simple, but make it tidy and aesthetically pleasing. That shows respect for the sacredness of your retreat time. Make sure you have a meditation cushion or a bench or chair to sit on. You might also want a small altar with sacred objects or images, a candle, and flowers.

Schedule: Decide what practices or activities you want to include in your retreat, and write them down on a schedule. You can find a variety of suggested schedules for self-retreats online. If you plan to meditate, try to structure it in periods of forty-five minutes or so. Alternate sitting with movement—walking meditation, perhaps, or a contemplative practice like yoga or tai chi. Consider setting aside time to listen to a guided meditation. Many Buddhist teachers have posted meditations on YouTube or Facebook or on their dedicated websites. This is an excellent way to learn a new practice or reach deep relaxation. A retreat is also a good time to listen to recorded Dharma talks—Buddhist teachings—or watch a video of a teacher. See the Resources section for suggestions on talks and meditations available for download, and also check the internet.

Meals: If you plan to eat one or more meals during your retreat, do the shopping beforehand. You could also prepare the meals in advance or, if you prefer, take this opportunity to practice mindful food prep. Keep the meals light so you won't feel sleepy. Have a supply of tea and juice and healthy snacks on hand.

Rest: Be sure to include rest time in your schedule. At most retreat centers, there is an hour or more of free time after meals when participants can rest or bathe or take a walk.

Chanting: Even if you've chosen to maintain silence during your retreat, you won't be violating the spirit of it by singing or chanting a mantra—sacred syllables. If you don't already know a mantra, you can find examples online or chant *Om mani padme hum* (page 139).

Journal: You may want to devote a little or a lot of your retreat time to writing in a journal. In any case, be sure to make notes on your practice and on any awareness you experience or issues that come up during the day.

PRACTICE: Letting Go

We don't have to take monastic vows to find peace in releasing what we no longer need or want. Some Buddhists are practicing renunciation by simplifying their lives mentally and materially. For some that involves downsizing and shedding possessions or reducing their footprint and monitoring how they consume. For others, it involves a change of mind or heart: letting go of unhealthy habits, outworn ideas, and energy-draining people and pursuits—and then filling their lives with positive attitudes and life-affirming people and activities.

PARTING THOUGHTS

Congratulations! You've covered the basics. Are you eager to try meditation or start a regular practice? Are you keen to dive deeper and explore? Or are you still wondering if Buddhism is for you?

Buddhism offers only a taste of the Buddhist teachings and practices, but I hope it has whetted your appetite to learn more. Buddhist history and Buddhadharma are rich enough to fill a lifetime—make that *lifetimes*—of study and practice. It is not a matter of adopting a new religion. I've been on Buddhist retreats where the participants included Catholic nuns and priests, Jewish rabbis, Protestant clergy, and others from a variety of spiritual traditions, as well as people identifying as atheists or agnostics. For years I wondered why one regular at our retreats always left a day early. Turned out he was a Presbyterian minister who had to drive several hundred miles to reach home in time to deliver a sermon on Sunday morning.

Buddhist practice is personal and pragmatic, and in the West today, increasingly non-sectarian. Ultimately it is about *you*. The Buddha set out on a journey of self-discovery, and when he found what he was seeking, he realized he was not alone in his quest. Nor are you. Whether curiosity, vague discontent, desperation, or dedication drives you, Buddhism can support you in realizing your true nature—or as a Zen master might say, in seeing your original face.

Have no fear that the journey will be a slog—an exercise in extreme self-discipline with dour task masters driving you toward awakening. Buddhist teachers include some of the liveliest and warmest spiritual guides you will ever meet. Humor abounds. Think of those ancient Zen masters with their zany stories, sly jokes, mind-bending koans, and laughter—all in the service of helping their students awaken.

The Dalai Lama serves as a sparkling example of how Buddhist practice makes each moment count, even when life brings us sorrow and pain. His famous sunny smile and hearty laugh are undiminished by the grave losses he has suffered and the challenges he faces daily as the spiritual leader of the Tibetan people. What a teaching on impermanence and acceptance that is! He's the embodiment of wisdom and compassion.

From the Theravadins we learn how to observe our moment-to-moment experience and disperse the clouds of affliction to reveal the clear sky of the enlightened mind. The Mahayana Buddhists introduce us to our Buddha nature and the bodhisattva path of dedication to awakening in order to help others. Vajrayana teaches us to embrace our passions and darkest moods as the fuel of transformation. Regardless of the *yana*—the vehicle of enlightenment—we choose, the path is the pursuit of truth. There's an old Zen saying: "Most people prefer chewing the menu to actually eating the food." We seekers are not most people. Nothing less than real food will satisfy us.

Often on the journey toward true happiness, the road is not straight. And the simplest lessons may be the most profound. Consider this observation from the seventeenth-century Japanese poet Mizuta Masahide:

Barn's burnt down—
now
I can see the moon.

Acknowledgments

Every writer dreams of having an editor like Joel Fotinos. Astute and creative, warm and supportive, he perfectly embodies the essence of a Buddha: wisdom and compassion. I've wanted to work with Joel since we met more than twenty years ago. It's an honor to be part of the Essential Wisdom series he is launching for St. Martin's.

Behind every good editor is a crackerjack team. Gwen Hawkes, Joel's intrepid assistant, has my everlasting gratitude. Cheerful and unflappable, she took delays in stride, smoothing the way for the book to proceed on schedule. My thanks also to the rest of the St. Martin's team: Eric C. Meyer, production editor; Mary Louise Mooney, copy editor; Kerri Resnick, jacket designer; Martin Quinn, marketing; and Alex Casement, publicist.

An unsung hero of this project is John House, an impeccable editor who gamely agreed to give the manuscript a last-minute read. John's incisive queries and suggestions, along with his knowledge of Buddhism, pushed me to dig deeper and make this a better book.

Profuse thanks to James Shaheen, editor and publisher of *Tricycle: The Buddhist Review*, and his staff. Along with *Tricycle* founder Helen Tworkov, they've graciously provided an editorial home and an ongoing education in Buddhadharma.

My dear friend Patty Gift, editorial director of Hay House, lent her expertise in many practical ways, along with friendship that carried me through bouts of writer's doubt.

A deep bow of gratitude to Marcy Vaughn, meditation teacher and mentor, along with Gabriel Rocca and Kallon Basquin of The 3 Doors. They've set a powerful example, and their teachings have been transforming, allowing me to finally integrate four decades of Buddhist practice.

To the 3 Doors sangha, my thanks for your friendship and support. I couldn't ask for a more enthusiastic cheerleader than Kathy Hayden, whose humor and encouragement have literally kept me going. For their courage and insights I thank my dharma sisters in the Monday group: Kathy, Elly Grace, Patti McIntyre, and Maggie Scobie.

Finally, I'm indebted to Dr. Hasan Asif, who found the perfect combination of neuroscience, psychology, and spirit to keep my brain fired up for the project.

Notes

Abbreviations:

BPS   Buddhist Publication Society, Kandy, Sri Lanka

BCBS   Barre Center for Buddhist Studies, Barre, MA

Introduction

xv "Nearly five hundred million people . . .": *The Global Religious Landscape*, Pew Research Center, December 18, 2012; and *The Changing Religious Landscape*, Pew Research Center, April 5, 2017. Retrieved from www.pewforum.org/2012/12/18/global-religious-landscape-buddhist/ and www.pewforum.org/2017/04/05/the-changing-global-religious-landscape/

1. The Buddha

4 "I lived . . .": Sukhamala Sutta [Refinement], *Anguttara Nikaya 3:39*, translated from the Pali by Thanissaro Bhikkhu (dhammatalks.org.) Retrieved from www.dhammatalks.org/suttas/AN/AN3_39.html.

4 "a white . . . dew": Sukhamala Sutta, *Anguttara Nikaya 3:39*, trans. Thanissaro Bhikkhu.

5 "I am supreme . . . for me": T. W. Rhys Davids, trans, *Buddhist*

Birth-stories, (Jataka-tales): The *Commentarial Introduction Entitled Nidana-Katha*, the *Story* of the *Lineage*, new and rev. edition T. W. Rhys Davids (New Delhi, Madras: Asian Educational Services, 1999), 155.

5 "and remove . . . world": T. W. Rhys Davids, *Buddhist Birth Stories*, 161.

9 "It isn't easy . . . shell": Maha-Saccaka Sutta [The Longer Discourse to Saccaka], *Majjhima Nikaya 36*, translated from the Pali by Thanissaro Bhikkhu (dhammatalks.org). Retrieved from www.dhammatalks.org/suttas/MN/MN36.html.

10 "spine . . . beads": Maha-Saccaka Sutta, *Majjhima Nikaya 36*, translated from the Pali by Thanissaro Bhikkhu.

11 "Wherefore . . . lusts: Sir Edwin Arnold, *The Light of Asia* (Create Space Independent Publishing Platform, 2013), 82.

11 "ten chief sins . . . hence": Arnold, *The Light of Asia*, 83.

11 "demon-armies": Arnold, *The Light of Asia*, 82.

11–12 Dialogue not previously cited was adapted from T. W. Rhys Davids, translator, *Buddhist Birth-Stories*, 195–96.

13 "a hundred thousand births": Bhikkhu Nanamoli, *The Life of the Buddha* (Seattle: BPS Pariyatti Editions, 1992), 23.

14 "The world is lost . . . destroyed": Ayacana Sutta [The Request] *Samyutta Nikaya 6:1*, translated from the Pali by Thanissaro Bhikkhu (dhammatalks.org). Retrieved from www.dhammatalks.org/suttas/SN/SN6_1.html.

14 "There are beings . . . understand [it]": Ayacana Sutta, trans. Thanissaro Bhikkhu.

16 "A sense . . . individuals": Dhammaññu Sutta [One with a Sense of Dhamma], *Anguttara Nikaya 7:64*, translated from the Pali by Thanissaro Bhikkhu (dhammatalks.org). Retrieved from https://dhammatalks.org/AN/AN7_64.html.

21 "That's . . . death": Jara Sutta [Old Age], *Samyutta Nikaya 48:41*, translated from the Pali by Thanissaro Bhikkhu (dhammatalks .org). Retrieved from www.dhammatalks.org/suttas/SN/SN48 _41.html.

2. Buddhism After the Buddha

28 "unique . . . religion": D. T. Suzuki, *An Introduction to Zen Buddhism.* (New York: Grove Press, 1964), 32.

29 "The deepest . . . intelligible": D. T. Suzuki, *An Introduction to Zen Buddhism,* 33.

29 "practical and systematic": D. T. Suzuki, *An Introduction to Zen Buddhism,* 34.

29 "more than . . . sense" *and* "The discipline . . . existence": D. T. Suzuki, *An Introduction to Zen Buddhism,* 40.

29 "mere waste . . . more": D. T. Suzuki, *An Introduction to Zen Buddhism,* 38–9.

30 "A monk . . . 'Mu'": *Two Zen Classics,* Katsuki Sekida, trans. (New York and Tokyo: Weatherhill, 1977), 27.

30 "the nature" and "To recognize . . . interpretation": Robert Aitken Roshi, "The Koan 'No'." Retrieved from boundlesswayzen.org/the -koan-no/, November 19, 2016.

31 "will be . . . try": Sekida, *Two Zen Classics,* 28.

31 "is not . . . ideologies": Roshi Joan Halifax, "Being Met by the Reality Called Mu" (2005). Retrieved from www.upaya.org/dox/Mu .pdf.

32 "To study . . . things": Dogen Zenji, "Genjo Koan," Reiho Masunaga, trans. In *Soto Approach to Zen,* chapter 9 (Tokyo: Layman Buddhist Society Press, 1958), 125–32.

32 "Dogen . . . transcended": Zoketsu Norman Fischer, "Zen Koan Practice Introduction, Who Hears This Sound?" Everyday Zen Foundation, May 13, 2001. Retrieved from http://everydayzen .org/teachings/2001/1-zen-koan-practice-introduction-who-hears -sound.

36 "One must . . . pleasure": Robert A. F. Thurman, *Wisdom and Compassion: The Sacred Art of Tibet* (New York: Harry N. Abrams, 1991), 27.

3. The Teachings

57 "What do you think . . . forest?" *and* "In the same . . . taught": Simsapa Sutta (The Simsapa Leaves), *Samyutta Nikaya 56.31,* translated from the Pali by Thanissaro Bhikkhu (dhammatalks.org). Retrieved from www.dhammatalks.org/suttas/SN/SN56_31.html.

62 "to the virtue . . . claim": Stephen Batchelor, *After Buddhism: Rethinking the Dharma for a Secular Age* (New Haven and London: Yale University Press, 2015), 117–8.

64 "As long . . . goes on": Walpola Rahula, *What the Buddha Taught,* rev. ed. (New York: Grove, 2007), 34.

65 "Vision . . . before": Dhammacakkapavattana Sutta [Setting the Wheel of Dhamma in Motion], *Samyutta Nikaya 56:11,* translated by Thanissaro Bhikkhu (dhammatalks.org). Retrieved from www.dhammatalks.org/suttas/SN/SN56_11.html.

66 "The Buddha . . . experientially": Andrew Olendzki, "A Noble Path," *Tricycle: The Duddhist Review* (Summer 2016), 32.

66 "Right . . . practice": Jack Kornfield, "Right Understanding." Retrieved from https://jackkornfield.com/right-understanding.

69 "In Buddhism . . . causes": The Dalai Lama, *From Here to Enlightenment: An Introduction to Tsong-kha-pa's Classic Text* The Great Treatise on the Stages of the Path to Enlightenment, Guy Newland, trans. (Boulder, CO: Snow Lion, 2014), 34.

70 "Happiness . . . . wisdom": The Dalai Lama, *From Here to Enlightenment,* 35.

71 "the source . . . desire": Walpola Rahula, *What the Buddha Taught,* 51.

72 "Very . . . chariot": T. W. Rhys Davids, trans. *The Questions of King Milinda,* Pt. I, Book II: Lakkhana Panha (The Distinguishing Characteristics of Ethical Qualities), Ch. 1, in *Sacred Books of the East,* Vol. XXXV (Oxford: Clarendon Press, 1890), 44. Retrieved from www.sacred-texts.com/bud/sbe35/sbe3504.htm#page_43.

75 "secretly . . . worlds": Reiho Masunaga, *A Primer of Soto Zen: A Translation of Dogen's Shobogenzo Zuimonki* (Honolulu: University of Hawaii Press, 1979), 19–20.

75 "I am the owner . . . heir": Upajjhatthana Sutta [Subjects for Con-

templation], *Anguttara Nikaya* 5.57, translated from the Pali by Thanissaro Bhikkhu (dhammatalks.org). Retrieved from www.dhammatalks.org/suttas/AN/AN5_57.html.

77 "Nirvana . . . itself": D. T. Suzuki, *Outlines of Mahayana Buddhism* (New York: Schocken Books, 1963), 355–56.

77 "Not knowing . . . imploringly": Hakuin Ekaku Zenji, "The Song of Zazen," translated by Eido Shimano Roshi, in *Daily Sutras for Chanting and Recitation,* edited by Shinge Roko Sherry Chayat Roshi (New York: Zen Studies Society, rev. ed. 2018), 23. Retrieved from www.zenstudies.org/wp-content/uploads/2018/02/ZSS-Sutra-Book .pdf.

77 "To search . . . exist": Bodhidharma, *The Zen Teaching of Bodhidharma,* trans. Red Pine (San Francisco: North Point Press, 1989), 9.

78 Quotes on the twelve links of dependent origination: Bhikkhu Khantipalo, "The Wheel of Birth and Death," *The Wheel* 147/148 /149 (BPS, 1970, 1995), from an article in *Visakha Puja* 251 (Bangkok: The Buddhist Association of Thailand, no date found), *Access to Insight (BCBS Edition),* November 30, 2013. Retrieved from www.accesstoinsight.org/lib/authors/khantipalo/wheel147.html.

85 "Whoever . . . sees the Buddha": N. Ross Reat, trans., *The Salistamba Sutra* (Delhi: Motilal Banarsidass, 1993), 27.

88 "a complex flow . . . patterns": His Holiness the Dalai Lama, introductory commentary to *The Tibetan Book of the Dead: First Complete Translation,* edited by Graham Coleman and Thupten Jinpa, translated by Gyurme Dorje (New York: Penguin Classics, 2007), xiii.

89 "If . . . mothers": Geshe Kelsang Gyatso, *Meaningful to Behold: The Bodhisattva's Way of Life* (Delhi: Motilal Banarsidass, 2000), 28.

90 "eight . . . around": Bhikkhu Bodhi, ed., "The Vicissitudes of Life (AN 8:6)," in *In the Buddha's Words: An Anthology of Discourses from the Pali Canon* (Boston: Wisdom, 2005), 32.

91 "The Buddhist . . . actions" *and* "Since . . . consequences": Martine Batchelor, "The Buddhist Precepts: An Introduction," *Tricycle: The Buddhist Review* (Winter 2003), 36.

91 "skillful . . . suffering" and "Sometimes . . . within": Martine Batchelor, "The Buddhist Precepts," 37.

95 "the misfortunes . . . madness": Bhikkhu Bodhi, "Going for Refuge & Taking the Precepts," *The Wheel* 282/284 (Kandy, Sri Lanka:
Buddhist Publication Society, 1981), *Access to Insight (BCBS Edition)*, December 1, 2013. Retrieved from www.accesstoinsight.org
/lib/authors/bodhi/wheel282.html.

96 "always . . . beings": *The Brahma Net Sutra*, translated by the Buddhist Text Translation Society. Retrieved www.fodian.net/world
/1484.html.

97 "the Buddha's primary . . . happiness": Thanissaro Bhikkhu,
Head & Heart Together: Bringing Wisdom to the Brahmaviharas
(dhammatalks.org, January 9, 2018). Retrieved from www
.dhammatalks.org/books/Head&HeartTogether/Section0011
.html.

97 "practices . . . others": Sharon Salzberg, *A Heart as Wide as the World:
Stories on the Path of Lovingkindness*, rev. ed. (Boston and London:
Shambhala, 1999), 30–31.

97 "Is there anyone . . . yourself?" *and* "Searching . . . love yourself":
Rājan Sutta [The King], *Udana 5:1*, translated from the Pali
by Thanissaro Bhikkhu (dhammatalks.org). Retrieved from
www.dhammatalks.org/suttas/KN/Ud/ud5_1.html.

98 "The mind . . . of all": Acharya Buddharakkhita, *Metta: The Philosophy and Practice of Universal Love* (Kandy, Sri Lanka: Buddhist Publishing Society, 1989, 2013; BPA Pariyatti edition, 2014).

100 "allows . . . disposal" *and* "[It] allows us . . . fear": Sharon Salzberg,
Lovingkindess: The Revolutionary Art of Happiness (Boston and London: Shambhala, 1997), 103.

100 "to acknowledge . . . exist": Salzberg, *Lovingkindess*, 104.

101 "all . . . attachment" *and* "share . . . goodness": Salzberg, *Lovingkindess*, 130.

102 "rejoicing . . . happiness": B. Alan Wallace, *The Four Immeasurables:
Cultivating a Boundless Heart* (Ithaca, NY, and Boulder, CO: Snow
Lion, 2004), 146.

102 "Recognize . . . it": Wallace, *The Four Immeasurables,* 147.

106 "Taking . . . universes": Chögyam Trungpa, "The Bodhisattva," *Lion's Roar,* January 1, 2017. Retrieved from www.lionsroar.com /the-bodhisattva/.

107 "to hold this . . . step": Pema Chödrön, *No Time to Lose: A Timely Guide to the Way of the Bodhisattva* (Boston and London: Shambhala, 2007), 69.

107 "However . . . follow it": Zen Studies Society, "Shigu Seigan" ("Great Vows for All"), in *Daily Sutras for Chanting and Recitation* (New York: Zen Studies Society, revised 2018), 16. Retrieved from www.zenstudies.org/wp-content/uploads/2018/02/ZSS-Sutra -Book.pdf.

108 "is simply . . . manifestation": Mu Soeng, *Heart of the Universe: Exploring the Heart Sutra* (Somerville, MA, Wisdom, 2010), 61.

108 "In the world . . . processes": Mu Soeng, *Heart of the Universe,* 39.

108 "Thus a more . . . emptiness": Mu Soeng, *Heart of the Universe,* 42.

110 "often . . . to it": Elizabeth Mattis-Namgyal, "The Beauty of Renunciation," *Lion's Roar* Forum, retrieved from www.lionsroar.com /forum-the-beauty-of-renunciation/

111 "Buddha . . . harmony": Robert Aitken Roshi, *The Mind of Clover: Essays in Zen Buddhist Ethics* (New York: North Point Press, 1984), 4.

112 "Not taking . . . person" *and* "but taking . . . life": Bhikkhu Bodhi, *Going for Refuge & Taking the Precepts.*

112 "inner states . . . all have" *and* "confidence . . . growth": Gil Fronsdal, "Going for Refuge," Retrieved from www.insightmeditation center.org/books-articles/going-for-refuge/.

113 "it . . . despair": Bhikkhu Bodhi, *Going for Refuge & Taking the Precepts.*

113 "Since . . . dejection," Bhikkhu Bodhi, *Going for Refuge & Taking the Precepts.*

113 "He was . . . egotism": Karen Armstrong, *Buddha* (New York: Penguin, 2001), xxviii.

115 "On a psychological . . . for years": Thubten Chodron, "Preliminary practice (ngondro) overview." Retrieved from https://thubten chodron.org/2009/09/clearing-and-enriching-mind/.

116 "to engender . . . ahead": Bruce Newman, *A Beginner's Guide to Tibetan Buddhism* (Ithaca, NY, and Boulder, CO: Snow Lion Publications, 2004), 33.

117 "an increasing . . . (emptiness)": Alexander Berzin, "Differences Among the Four Classes of Tantra," studybuddhism.com. Retrieved from https://studybuddhism.com/en/advanced-studies/vajrayana /tantra-theory/the-differences-among-the-four-classes-of-tantra.

118 "Tantrism . . . delusion": Traleg Kyabgon, *The Essence of Buddhism: An Introduction to Its Philosophy and Practice* (Boston and London: Shambhala), 147.

118 "The way . . . wisdoms": Traleg Kyabgon, *The Essence of Buddhism*, 147.

4. The Practices

120 "The attainment . . . sees it": Kitagiri Sutta [At Kitagiri], *Majjhima Nikaya 70*, translated from the Pali by Thanissaro Bhikkhu (dhammatalks.org). Retrieved from www.dhamatalks.org/suttas/MN /MN70.html.

121 "begin the long . . . behavior": Thanissaro Bhikkhu, *Dhamma*, Access to Insight (BCBS edition). Retrieved from www.accesstoinsight .org/ptf/dhamma/index.html.

121 "the basic . . . self": Thanissaro Bhikkhu, trans., *Dhamma*.

122 "Just as . . . views": Pema Chödrön, *Living Beautifully with Uncertainty and Change* (Boston and London: Shambhala, 2012), 42.

122 "Creating . . . justice": Dr. Jay Michaelson, "Jhana: The Spice Your Meditation Has Been Missing," *Trike Daily*, September 22, 2016, www.tricycle.org.

122 "aims . . . Nirvana": Rahula, *What the Buddha Taught*, 68.

123 "producing . . . tranquility": Rahula, *What the Buddha Taught*, 67.

123 "Sit . . . easy" *and* "The spine . . . manner": Bhante Henepola Gunaratana, *Mindfulness in Plain English*, (Boston: Wisdom Publications, 2011, 2015), 58.

124 "After . . . joy": Thich Nhat Hanh, *The Miracle of Mindfulness: An Introduction to the Practice of Mindfulness* (Boston: Beacon, 1999), 35.

125 "Mindfulness . . . mind": Joseph Goldstein, *One Dharma: The Emerging Western Buddhism* (San Francisco, HarperSanFrancisco, 2002), 13.

125 "Mindfulness . . . non-judgmentally": Jon Kabat-Zinn, *Wherever You Go, There You Are: Mindfulness in Everyday Life* (New York: Hachette Books, 10th ed., 2005), 4.

125 "faculty . . . interruption": Gunaratana, *Mindfulness in Plain English*, 144.

125 "a delicate . . . sensibilities": Gunaratana, *Mindfulness in Plain English*, 143.

126 "a calm . . . wisdom": Bhante Gunaratana, *The Jhanas in Theravada Buddhist Meditation* (BPS, 1988), 1.

128 "insight . . . mind": Rahula, *What the Buddha Taught*, 68.

128 "It is . . . observation" and "the most important . . . development": Rahula, *What the Buddha Taught*, 69.

129 "the wandering mind . . . alone" *and* "It . . . 'wandering'": Venerable Mahasi Sayadaw, "Satipatthana Vipassana," *The Wheel* 370/371 (BPS, 1990), *Access to Insight (BCBS Edition),* June 3, 2010. Retrieved from www.accesstoinsight.org/lib/authors/mahasi/wheel370.html.

129 "Insight knowledge . . . happening": Venerable Mahasi Sayadaw, "Thoughts on the Dhamma by the Venerable Mahasi Sayadaw, Selected from His Discourses," *The Wheel* 298/300 (BPS, 1983), *Access to Insight (BCBS Edition),* November 30, 2013. Retrieved from www.accesstoinsight.org/lib/authors/mahasi/wheel298.html.

129 "Watch . . . lightning" *and* "if you . . . happen": Venerable Mahasi Sayadaw, *A Discourse on "To Nibbana Via the Noble Eightfold Path," Inclusive of "Saraniya Dhamma" & "Mahapaccavekkhana,"* translated by U Htin Fatt, new edition edited by Bhikkhu Pesala (Socialist Republic of the Union of Burma, 1980, 2013). Retrieved from www .aimwell.org/To%20Nibbana%20Via%20the%20Noble%20Eightfold%20Path.pdf.

129 "In vipassana . . . name": Mahasi Sayadaw, "Satipatthana Vipassana."

131 "eight . . . previous": Leigh Brasington, "A Mind Pure, Concentrated, and Bright," interview by Mary Talbot, *Tricycle: The Buddhist Review,* Winter 2004, 67.

131   "Throughout . . . now": Gunaratana, *The Jhanas*, 3.

134   "we gently . . . others": Salzberg, *Lovingkindness*, 29–30.

134   "is not . . . luxury" *and* "but . . . struggle": Sharon Salzberg and Robert Thurman, *Love Your Enemies: How to Break the Anger Habit & Be a Whole Lot Happier* (Carlsbad, CA: Hay House, 2013), 161.

135   "It is . . . appointment": Salzberg and Thurman, *Love Your Enemies*, 161.

136   "Practicing . . . cruelty": Salzberg and Thurman, *Love Your Enemies*, 163.

137   "the unspoken . . . spirit": Salzberg and Thurman, *Love Your Enemies*, 165.

138   "Altruistic . . . torments": Matthieu Ricard, *Altruism: The Power of Compassion to Change Yourself and the World* (Boston: Little, Brown and Company, 2015), 266.

139   "that . . . world"; "Imagine . . . universe"; and "you . . . homeless: Ricard, *Altruism*, 267.

141   "overgrowths . . . insight": Nyanaponika Thera, ed., trans., "The Five Mental Hindrances and Their Conquest: Selected Texts from the Pali Canon and Commentaries," *The Wheel* 26 (BPS, 1993), *Access to Insight (BCBS Edition)*, November 30, 2013. Retrieved from www.accesstoinsight.org/lib/authors/nyanaponika/wheel026.html.

142   "often . . . away" *and* "physically . . . motivationally": Insight Meditation Center, "Introduction to Mindfulness Meditation: The Five Hindrances." Retrieved from http://insightmeditationcenter.org /articles/FiveHindrances.pdf.

142   "RAIN . . . experience": Tara Brach, *True Refuge: Finding Peace and Freedom in Your Own Awakened Heart* (New York: Bantam, 2013), 62.

142   "You can awaken . . . right now?": Brach, *True Refuge*, 63.

142   "with investigation . . . inquiry": Brach, *True Refuge*, 64.

142   "We need . . . kindness '": Brach, *True Refuge*, 65.

143   "We do not reject . . . there" *and* "we . . ."face": Ringu Tulku, *Daring Steps: Traversing the Path of the Buddha*, 2nd ed. (Ithaca, NY, and Boulder, CO: Snow Lion, 2010), 133.

143 "Don't recall . . . and rest": "Tilopa's Six Nails," translated by Kenneth McLeod, *Unfettered Mind: Pragmatic Buddhism* website. Retrieved from http://unfetteredmind.org/tilopas-advice/.

145 "walking . . . make": Thich Nhat Hanh, *Present Moment, Wonderful Moment: Mindfulness Verses for Daily Living* (Berkeley, CA: Parallax Press, 2nd ed., 2002), 57.

152 "Barn's . . . moon": Mizuta Masahide, "Barn's burnt down," in *Zen Poetry: Let the Spring Breeze Enter*, Lucien Stryk and Takashi Ikemoto, trans. (New York: Grove Press, 1995), 77.

Glossary

Note: Sanskrit is hyphenated as Skt.

anatta (anatman, Skt.): "non-self," "not-self," "selflessness," "egolessness"—doctrine denying there is a separately existing, permanent, intrinsic self. One of the Three Marks of Existence, or conditioned reality, along with *dukkha*, suffering, and *anicca*, impermanence.

anicca (anitya, Skt.): impermanence. One of the Three Marks of Existence, along with *dukkha*, suffering, and *anatta*, non-self.

arahant (arhat, Skt.): "accomplished one," person who has attained nirvana—liberation from cyclic existence.

bardo (Tibetan): transitional state between life and death

bhikkhu, Pali (bhiksu, Skt.): Buddhist monk

bhikkhuni (bhikksuni, Skt.): Buddhist nun

bodhi, Skt./Pali: awakening. The Bodhi tree is the ficus tree under which the Buddha sat on the night of his enlightenment.

bodhicitta, Skt.: mind of awakening

bodhisattva (bodhisatta, Pali): one with the altruistic aspiration to awaken in order to benefit all beings

Bön: ancient indigenous spiritual tradition of Tibet; has much in common with Tibetan Buddhism

Brahma Viharas, Pali: four "heavenly abodes" attained through developing *metta* (loving-kindness), *karuna* (compassion), *mudita* (sympathetic joy), and *upekkha* (equanimity)

Brahmin: priestly class, the highest caste in India in the Buddha's time

Buddha: Awakened One

The Buddhacarita (Acts of the Buddha): epic biography by first-century CE Indian Buddhist philosopher Asvaghosa

Buddhadharma (Buddhadhamma, Pali): teachings of the Buddha

Buddha nature: the innate qualities of a Buddha enabling all sentient beings to attain enlightenment.

chakravartin, Pali: wheel-turner or universal ruler

Chan Buddhism: Mahayana school introduced to China in fifth century CE. Later spread to Japan as Zen, Korea as Seon, and Vietnam as Thièn.

citta, Skt./Pali: mind, heart

dependent origination: also dependent co-arising. Chain of causation that binds us to suffering. Holds that everything is relative and interconnected, and does not arise independent of conditions. Often characterized by the phrases *When this is, that is. When this arises, that arises. When this is not, that is not. When this ceases, that ceases.*

deva: heavenly being

Dharma (Dhamma, Pali): from root *dham*, to uphold. In a broad sense means law, principle, truth, or fundamental law of existence. More specifically, the teachings and practices taught by the Buddha and his followers.

dharmadhatu, Skt.: *dhatu* is "realm, sphere, essence"; dharmadhatu means the realm of a buddha.

dhyana, Skt.: meditation or meditative absorption

dukkha, Pali: suffering, dissatisfaction; one of the Three Marks of Existence, along with *anatta* (non-self) and *anicca* (impermanence)

empowerment: in Vajrayana, an initiation conferring permission to perform certain tantric practices

Engaged Buddhism: application of Buddhist insights and teachings to social, political, economic, and environmental issues and injustice

enlightenment: nirvana, awakening, realization

Four Noble Truths: central teaching of the Buddha: (1) the existence of suffering; (2) the origin of suffering; (3) the cessation of suffering; (4) the path to cessation of suffering

Four Sights: encounters with old age, sickness, death, and a sadhu or wandering monk that led Siddhartha Gautama to seek the end of suffering

ganachakra, Skt.: ritual feast in Tibetan Buddhism

guru, Skt. (lama, Tibetan): spiritual teacher or mentor

jhana, Pali: meditative absorption, or state of strong concentration

karma (kamma, Pali): intentional action; law of cause and effect

karuna, Pali: compassion, one of the four Brahma Viharas

klesha, Pali: defilement, such as greed, anger, and delusion

Kshatriya, Skt.: warrior class, second-highest caste in India of the Buddha's day; Gautama family were members

The Lalivastara (Play in Full): third century CE Mahayana Buddhist sutra recounting the Buddha's early days

lama, Tibetan (guru, Skt.): spiritual teacher or mentor; in Tantra, ritual master.

Madhyamaka: doctrine of the Middle Way; one of two principal schools of Mahayana Buddhism, along with Yogacara

Mahayana Buddhism: "Great Vehicle"; teachings of the Bodhisattva path

mandala, Skt.: sacred diagram used as a meditation object

mantra, Skt.: short verse or sacred syllables chanted as a meditation object or to evoke a deity

Mara: "The Tempter"; demon who personifies death and rebirth, and the passions that bind us to *samsara*

Metta, Pali: loving-kindness, one of the four Brahma Viharas

Middle Way: path of moderation between extremes of self-indulgence and self-mortification

mudita, Pali: sympathetic joy, one of the four Brahma Viharas

mudra: ritual hand gesture

ngondro (Tibetan): preliminary practices

Nidana-Katha (Jataka Tales): stories of the Buddha's previous lives as a bodhisattva

nirvana (nibbana, Pali): "blowing out," or extinguishing of the fires of greed, anger, and delusion; liberation, the goal of Buddhist practice

Noble Eightfold Path: Middle Way, or path of practice to cessation of suffering

Pali: North Indian dialect similar to that spoken by the Buddha; language of the earliest Buddhist discourses

Pali Canon: "Teachings of the Elders," earliest records of the Buddha's discourses

paramita (parami, Pali): perfection of character.

parinirvana (parinibbana, Pali): final nirvana of a Buddha or enlightened person, after which there will be no more rebirth

precepts: vows or guidelines given by the Buddha to help us refrain from harmful action

roshi: honorific for Zen master

sadhu: wandering ascetic, holy man

Sakyamuni: "Sage of the Sakyas," epithet for the Buddha

samadhi (samapatti, Pali): deep concentration

samsara, Skt.: cyclic existence

Sangha: community of followers of the Buddha and Buddhadharma; one of the Three Jewels, along with the Buddha and the Dharma

sankhara (samskara, Skt.): formation

sati, Pali: mindfulness

satori (Japanese): sudden enlightenment

shamatha (samatha, Skt.): calm abiding; one-pointed concentration practice

Shudra: laborers, fourth and lowest caste in India of the Buddha's day

shunyata (sunnata, Pali): emptiness

sila, Pali: virtue, morality

skandha (khanda, Pali): "heap," "mass," "aggregate." Five skandhas together constitute a living being.

sutra (sutta, Pali): literally, "thread." Buddhist teaching, usually a sermon or discourse by the Buddha or one of his followers.

tantras, Skt.: esoteric Indian scriptures central to Vajarayana practice

Tathagata, Pali: "Thus gone" or "Thus come," referring to the Buddha after enlightenment

Ten Qualities of a Buddha: *paramitas* (*paramis* Pali), qualities developed over lifetimes by a bodhisattva. In the Theravada tradition: generosity, virtue, renunciation, wisdom, persistence/energy, patience, truthfulness, determination, kindness, equanimity. In the Mahayana tradition, there are six qualities: generosity, morality, patience, perseverance/energy, meditative concentration, wisdom.

terma: Tibetan treasure texts hidden to be discovered later by *tertons*, treasure revealers

Theravada: Teaching of the Elders, the earliest Buddhist school

Theravadin: one who follows the Teachings of the Elders

The Three Jewels: Buddha, Dharma, and Sangha; also known as the Three Refuges

Three Marks of Existence: three characteristics of samsara, or conditioned existence: *dukkha* (suffering), *anatta* (non-self), and *anicca* (impermanence)

Three Poisons: attachment, aversion, and ignorance (alternatively: greed, anger, and delusion), the source of all suffering, according to the Buddha

Tipitaka (Tripitaka, Skt.): "Three Baskets," the three main divisions of the Pali Canon: the *Vinaya* (monastic code of discipline), the *Suttana* (discourses), and the *Abhidhamma* (systematic analysis of the teachings in the suttas; also known as Buddhist Psychology)

upaya, Skt.: skillful means, the Buddha's special teaching technique

upekkha, Pali: equanimity, one of the four Brahma Viharas

Vaishya, Skt.: third caste in India of the Buddha's day, consisting of farmers and merchants

Vajrayana, Skt.: Diamond Vehicle, the third major Buddhist tradition, commonly known as Tibetan Buddhism

Vinaya, Pali: rules of monastic discipline; one of three divisions of the Pali Canon

Vipassana (Vipashyana, Skt.): Insight meditation, from *vipassana*, Pali for "clear insight"

yana: "vehicle," referring to mode of practice conveying one to awakening. In Buddhism it specifically refers to the three main schools: Hinayana ("Lesser Vehicle"), outmoded term for Theravada; Mahayana ("Great Vehicle"); and Vajrayana ("Diamond Vehicle").

Yogacara, Skt.: one of two principal schools of Mahayana Buddhism, along with Madhyamaka

zabuton, Japanese: square black floor cushion for meditation

zafu, Japanese: round black meditation cushion

zazen, Japanese: Zen meditation

Zen Buddhism: Originally Chan, or Chinese Buddhism, Mahayana school introduced to Japan in the twelfth century CE

zendo, Japanese: Zen meditation hall

Resources

You've read the book. Now you'd like to learn more, maybe even find a practice center near you or go on a meditation retreat. Here is a sampling of resources for taking a deeper dive into Buddhism and Buddhist practice.

Local Meditation Centers

Nearly every community has Buddhist centers that offer meditation instruction and regular group practice. See **buddhanet.info/wbd/** or **directory.lionsroar.com** for meditation centers in your area. Many have introductory programs for newcomers.

Retreat Centers

Retreat centers are the sleepaway camps of Buddhism, where, depending on the center, you can experience a meditation retreat for a weekend, a few days, or a week or more, or immerse yourself in an advanced training lasting several months. Contact the center's office for a retreat schedule and advice on the best retreat for you. See **buddhanet.info/wbd/** for a listing of Dharma centers worldwide.

Here are a few well-known residential retreat centers in America where you can learn meditation and study Buddhism:

Dai Bosatsu Zendo Kongo-ji
223 Beecher Lake Road
Livingston Manor, NY 12758
845-439-4566
office@daibosatsu.org
zenstudies.org/dai-bosatsu-zendo/
DESCRIPTION: *Workshops, Zen meditation retreats, and three-month kessei, or formal monastic training at a Rinzai Zen monastery in the Catskill Mountains.*

Green Gulch Farm Zen Center, Soryu-ji (Green Dragon Temple)
1601 Shoreline Highway
Muir Beach, CA 94965
415-383-3134 (information); 888-743-9362 (registration)
ggfoffice@sfzc.org
sfzc.org/green-gulch
DESCRIPTION: *Zen meditation retreats, study, and practice at a Soto Zen center and farm in Marin County, north of San Francisco. Affiliate of San Francisco Zen Center.*

Insight Meditation Society—The Retreat Center
1230 Pleasant Street
Barre, MA 01005
978-355-4378
rc@dharma.org
dharma.org
DESCRIPTION: Residential retreats in *Vipassana (Insight)* and *Metta (Loving-kindness)* meditation, and three-month intensive residential retreats.

Nyingma Institute
1815 Highland Place
Berkeley, CA 94709
510-809-1000
nyingmainstitute.com

DESCRIPTION: *Tibetan Buddhist retreats, courses, workshops including meditation and Kum Nye Tibetan yoga.*

San Francisco Zen Center
300 Page Street
San Francisco, CA 94102
415-863-3136
sfzc.org
DESCRIPTION: *Soto Zen meditation practice and study, residential training program, and guest rooms.*

Shambhala Mountain Center
151 Shambhala Way
Red Feather Lakes, CO 80545
888-788-7221 or 970-881-4230
frontdesk@shambhalamountain.org
shambhalamountain.org
DESCRIPTION: *Meditation and mindfulness retreats in Vajrayana and other Buddhist traditions.*

Spirit Rock Meditation Center
5000 Sir Francis Drake Boulevard
PO Box 169
Woodacre, CA 94973
415-488-0164
srmc@spiritrock.org
spiritrock.org
DESCRIPTION: *Residential and nonresidential retreats and programs in Vipassana (Insight) and Metta (Loving-kindness) meditation.*

Tassajara Zen Mountain Center
39171 Tassajara Road
Carmel Valley, CA 93924

415-865-1895 (guest season information); 888-743-9362 (guest season reservations)

sfzc.org/tassajara

DESCRIPTION: *Soto Zen monastic training (fall and winter); summer guest stays and study weeks. Affiliate of San Francisco Zen Center.*

Websites

The internet contains a wealth of information on everything from Buddhist teachings and teachers to retreat centers, meditation instruction, Dharma courses, practice tools, and books. For the teaching schedule, teachings, and practices of an individual teacher, search by the teacher's name.

Some sites to check out:

Access to Insight (accesstoinsight.org): Extensive library of texts and teachings from the Theravada tradition. Includes translations of more than 1,000 suttas—texts of the Buddha's discourses—along with classic Dharma books; study guides on themes like karma, nonviolence, and the Four Noble Truths; and basic meditation instruction.

Buddhanet (buddhanet.net): Stop #1 on the digital Buddhism tour, with the most extensive collection of Buddhist information online, including teachings and practices from the three main Buddhist traditions, as well as useful tools such as guided meditation audios and a comprehensive directory of Buddhist organizations and retreat centers worldwide. The "Buddhist Studies" section covers basic teachings, while the "Online Study Guide" offers a graduated course on the historical Buddha, his teachings, and Buddhist history and culture.

Buddhist Studies WWW Virtual Library (ciolek.com/wwwvl -buddhism.html): Tracks information on facilities and websites in the fields of Buddhism and Buddhist studies. The design is very "old web," but after more than two decades, it's still a good resource.

Buddha Weekly (buddhaweekly.com): Online magazine that has been publishing since 2007, with features, interviews, and videos on Buddhist teachings, teachers, practice, and application to daily life. Viewpoints of Theravada, Mahayana, and Vajrayana traditions represented.

The Buddhist Channel (buddhistchannel.tv): Global site dedicated to Buddhist news and features. Comprehensive coverage of latest issues and Buddhist activities around the world. Includes reviews, podcasts, interviews, practices, Dharma courses, and RSS news feed for daily updates.

Buddhist Peace Fellowship (buddhistpeacefellowship.org): Founded in 1978 as a catalyst for nonviolent, socially engaged Buddhism. Building on the interconnectedness of all things, BPF promotes social justice, peace, and economic and environmental sustainability. Website offers information on group activities and community building worldwide, as well as online courses.

dhammatalks.org (dhammatalks.org): Extensive collection of talks, writings, and English translations of suttas and other texts, including free downloads. The principal speaker, author, and translator is Thanissaro Bhikkhu, a monk in the Thai Forest tradition of Theravada Buddhism, who is abbot of Metta Forest Monastery in California.

Dharma Seed (dharmaseed.org): Online resource with audio of more than 25,000 talks and meditations related to Insight Meditation and associated practices, recorded at centers like the Insight Meditation Society, Spirit Rock, Gaia House in the UK, and New York Insight. A treasure trove of Theravadan teachings, available free for listening or download.

The Guardian (theguardian.com/world/buddhism): News and views on Buddhism around the world today. An intelligent look at how the teachings come alive for people in everyday situations.

His Holiness the Dalai Lama (dalailama.com/news): Website of the spiritual leader of the Tibetan people and one of the most revered and beloved religious figures in the world today. Blog follows the peripatetic teacher as he carries his message of compassion and nonviolence to a fractious world.

Lion's Roar (lionsroar.com): Website of the magazines *Lion's Roar* (formerly *Shambhala Sun*) and *Buddhadharma: The Practitioner's Quarterly*. Teachings from Shambhala founder Chögyam Trungpa Rinpoche, along with articles and interviews featuring popular contemporary teachers like Ani Pema Chödrön and leading voices from all Buddhist traditions. Includes useful guide to retreat centers in the United States and Canada.

Mindful (mindful.org): Online presence of the bimonthly magazine *Mindful*, the self-described "voice of the emerging mindfulness community." Articles on mindful living, mind-body health, and mindfulness at work, along with basic meditation instruction.

Secular Buddhist Association (secularbuddhism.org/): Basic instruction and guided meditations from a group that espouses "a natural, pragmatic approach" to the Buddha's teachings, "seeking to provide a framework for personal and social development within the cultural context of our time."

Sounds True (soundstrue.com): Multimedia publishing company with audio library of Buddhist teachings by teachers like Pema Chödrön, Jack Kornfield, Tara Brach, Reginald Ray, and Jon Kabat-Zinn. Online catalog.

Thich Nhat Hanh (tnhaudio.org): From the beloved Vietnamese Zen master, recordings of Dharma talks and retreats at his international practice center, Plum Village in southern France, and other venues around the world.

Tricycle (tricycle.org): Online home of the quarterly magazine *Tricycle: The Buddhist Review,* the leading independent voice of Buddhism in the West. Website offers Daily Dharma and Trike Daily blog, as well as webcasts, articles, interviews, Dharma talks, courses, and guided meditations featuring popular Buddhist teachers and scholars. Subscribers have access to additional material, including video teachings, monthly films, ebooks, community events, and twenty-seven years of wisdom archived from the magazine.

YouTube (youtube.com): This vast video-sharing service continually posts video teachings and meditation instruction by well-known teachers from all Buddhist traditions. The extensive offerings range from a Buddhism for Beginners track to archival footage of great masters of the past, including Mahasi Sayadaw, S. N. Goenka, Shunryu Suzuki Roshi, Chögyam Rinpoche, and Kalu Rinpoche. Contemporary teachers include the Dalai Lama, Pema Chödrön, Bhante Gunaratana, Jetsun Tenzin Palmo, Thich Nhat Hanh, Norman Fischer, and many more.

Magazines and Journals

Buddhadharma: The Practitioner's Quarterly (lionsroar.com/buddha dharma): Quarterly journal for practitioners established in 2002, published by Lion's Roar Foundation. Articles on Buddhist teachings and practice representing all Buddhist schools. Print and digital editions.

Lion's Roar: Buddhist Wisdom for Our Time (lionsroar.com /lionsroar-magazine): Bimonthly magazine (formerly *Shambhala Sun*) offering "independent, nonsectarian view of Buddhism, Culture, Meditation, and Life." Print and digital editions.

Mandala Magazine (fpmt.org/mandala): Biannual publication of the Foundation for the Preservation of the Mahayana Tradition. News, articles, and teachings from the Lama Yeshe and Lama Zopa Rinpoche archives. Print and digital editions.

Mindful (mindful.org/magazine): Bimonthly magazine, "the voice of the emerging mindfulness community," published by the Foundation for a Mindful Society. Print and digital editions.

Muryoko: Journal of Shin Buddhism (nembutsu.info): Online magazine of Pure Land Buddhism, with articles, reviews, and Dharma talks.

Tricycle: The Buddhist Review (tricycle.org/magazine): Quarterly magazine, founded in 1991, the leading independent journal of Buddhism in the West. Disseminates Buddhist teachings and practices, views and values, with a focus on establishing a dialogue between Buddhism and the wider culture. Print and digital editions.

Meditation Apps

Aura (aurahealth.io): Daily, personalized, three-minute meditation—different every day—plus "Mindful Breather" feature. Free. iOS and Android.

Buddhify (buddhify.com): Meditation and mindfulness practices to do on the go. $30/yr. iOS and Android.

Calm (calm.com): Choice of meditations from 3 to 30 minutes long, plus 7- and 21-day programs. $12.99/mo; $59.99/yr. iOS and Android.

Headspace (headspace.co): Top-rated guided-meditation app with clear instructions. Good for newbies and all levels. "Basics" pack of 10 meditations is followed by the "Basics 2" and "Basics 3" series and "Pro" level. $12.99/mo; $95.88/yr. iOS and Android.

Insight Timer (insighttimer.com): More than 12,000 guided meditations from over 2,000 teachers, plus talks and podcasts. Timer for nonguided meditations, plus calming ambient sounds. Community of more than five million meditators. Free. iOS and Android.

The Mindfulness App (themindfulnessapp.com): Introduction to mindfulness with guided and silent meditations from 3 to 30 minutes, plus customized mindfulness reminders throughout the day. $9.99/mo.; $59.99/yr. iOS and Android.

10% Happier (10percenthappier.com): Based on Dan Harris's book of the same name. Mindful meditations and courses guided by top teachers, including Sharon Salzberg, Joseph Goldstein, and George Mumford. 10-day free trial. $7.99/mo. iOS and Android.

Zenso Meditation Timer (https://itunes.apple.com/us/app/zenso -meditation-timer/id590280866?mt=8): A simple timer with a twist: it counts down the time by drawing an animated Zen *enso* (circle) as the session progresses, so you can see at a glance how much time has elapsed. (There's also an optional digital timer.) Choice of different bells, gongs, and singing bowls to sound the start and end of the meditation period, as well as a vibrate option. Free. iOS.

Basic Buddhist Bookshelf

In the past few decades, the Buddhist library has grown exponentially, and now there are hundreds of helpful and inspiring books by contemporary teachers. If you are new to Buddhism or just starting a Buddhist practice, here are a few modern classics and other books we recommend:

The Art of Happiness: A Handbook for Living, by His Holiness the Dalai Lama with Howard C. Cutler, M.D. (Riverhead Books, 10th anniversary ed., 2009): The purpose of life is to be happy, His Holiness says in this inspiring book that radiates his characteristic warmth and humor. Based on conversations with Dr. Cutler, a psychiatrist, the text explores how to overcome obstacles like anger and anxiety and find inner peace amid the pressures of modern life. *How to Practice: The Way to a Meaningful Life*, also by His Holiness (Atria Books, 2003), offers basic teachings and practices on meditation, wisdom, and morality. *An Open Heart:*

Practicing Compassion in Everyday Life (Back Bay Books, reprint ed., 2002) is the Dalai Lama's practical introduction to the Buddhist path.

Awakening the Buddha Within: Tibetan Wisdom for the Western World, by **Lama Surya Das** (Broadway Books, reprint ed., 1998): User-friendly guide to practicing the Buddha's Noble Eightfold Path by an American-born Tibetan Buddhist lama who, though trained in Asia, writes in a hip, humorous voice geared to Westerners. Also by Surya Das, *Buddha Is as Buddha Does: The Ten Original Practices for Enlightened Living* (HarperSanFrancisco, 2007), a guide to developing the paramitas—the qualities of a Buddha—in everyday life. If you're not yet sold on Buddhism, *Awakening to the Sacred: Creating a Personal Spiritual Life* (Harmony, reprint ed., 2000) integrates Buddhist practices with teachings from other wisdom traditions.

Blue Jean Buddha: Voices of Young Buddhists, edited by **Sumi Loundon Kim** (Wisdom, 2001): Fresh perspectives on Dharma practice from 28 Buddhists, nearly all under 30. The author, then Buddhist chaplain at Duke University and now Yale, followed up with *The Buddha's Apprentices: More Voices of Young Buddhists* (Wisdom, 2005), observations on Buddhist practice from high school and college students, with input from popular teachers Sharon Salzberg, Thich Nhat Hanh, and Surya Das.

Buddhism Without Beliefs: A Contemporary Guide to Awakening, by **Stephen Batchelor** (Riverhead, reprint ed., 1998): A lucid guide to Buddhist teachings with appeal for non-Buddhists and newbies. The author is a former Zen and Tibetan Buddhist monk who focuses on the Buddha's pragmatic approach as well-suited to contemporary secular life.

Dharma Punx, by **Noah Levine** (HarperOne, reprint ed., 2004): The author's hard-won transformation from angry, hard-drinking-and-drugging punk rocker to Buddhist teacher and recovery counselor—chronicled in this memoir—spawned Dharma Punx, a Buddhism-inflected big-tent movement offering meditation practice and community to the spiritually disaffected.

The Empty Mirror: Experiences in a Japanese Zen Monastery (St. Martin's, 1999) and *A Glimpse of Nothingness: Experiences in an American Zen Community* (St. Martin's Griffin, 2014): Instructive and absorbing memoirs by Dutch crime novelist Janwillem van de Wetering detailing the challenges and rewards of traditional Zen training.

The Experience of Insight: A Simple and Direct Guide to Buddhist Meditation, by Joseph Goldstein (Shambhala, reissue ed., 1987): Basic meditation instruction and what to expect on a retreat, from one of the teachers who introduced Vipassana (Insight) meditation to the West. Goldstein's *One Dharma: The Emerging Western Buddhism* (HarperOne, reprint ed., 2003) describes a new, integrated Buddhism on the rise in America that draws on commonalities among the three major traditions.

The Heart of the Buddha's Teaching, by **Thich Nhat Hanh** (Broadway Books, new ed., 1999): "Studying the basics of Buddhism under Zen master Thich Nhat Hanh is like learning basketball from Michael Jordan," one reviewer wrote. A beloved teacher, Thây, as he's called, has delivered his compassionate message in more than 100 books. Perennial favorites include *The Miracle of Mindfulness: An Introduction to the Practice of Meditation* (Beacon, 1999), *Zen Keys: A Guide to Zen Practice* (Harmony, reissue ed., 1994), and *Being Peace* (Parallax, 2nd ed., 2005).

The Jewel Tree of Tibet: The Enlightenment Engine of Tibetan Buddhism, by **Robert Thurman** (Atria Books, reprint ed., 2006): Teachings on Tibetan Buddhism and the path to enlightenment shared by all Buddhist traditions, based on a retreat taught by a charismatic teacher and noted professor. Other nonacademic books by Thurman worth exploring include *Love Your Enemies: How to Break the Anger Habit & Be a Whole Lot Happier* (Hay House, 2013), coauthored with Sharon Salzberg, and *Infinite Life: Awakening to Bliss Within* (Riverhead Books, 2005), coauthored with the Dalai Lama, which gives practical teachings on seven transcendent virtues: wisdom, generosity, justice, patience, creativity, contemplation, and making art in the service of others.

Lovingkindness: The Revolutionary Art of Happiness, by **Sharon Salzberg** (Shambhala, 2018): Classic work by the world-renowned teacher who introduced Metta (loving-kindness) practice to Westerners. Warmth and relatable teachings fill all her books, including *A Heart as Wide as the World: Stories on the Path of Lovingkindness* (Shambhala, rev. ed., 1999), *Real Happiness: The Power of Meditation: A 28-Day Program* (Workman, 2010), and *Real Love: The Art of Mindful Connection* (Flatiron Books, 2017). *Faith: Trusting Your Own Deepest Experience* (Riverhead Books, reissue ed., 2003) is Salzberg's frank—and personal—examination of the suffering that drives people to Buddhist practice.

Mindfulness in Plain English, by **Bhante Henepola Gunaratana** (Wisdom, anniversary ed., 2011): One of the bestselling and most influential books on mindfulness, called "a masterpiece" by Buddhist teacher Jon Kabat-Zinn. The author, a Theravadan monk, brings practice alive for meditators at all levels, especially newcomers. Follow-ups include *Beyond Mindfulness in Plain English: An Introductory Guide to Deeper States of Meditation* (Wisdom, 2009) and *Loving-Kindness in Plain English: The Practice of Metta* (Wisdom, 2017).

The Myth of Freedom and the Way of Meditation, by **Chögyam Trungpa** (Shambhala Classics, 2002): Modern classic by the brilliant and controversial Tibetan Buddhist tulku on how meditation can help us overcome destructive patterns and discover true freedom. *Cutting Through Spiritual Materialism* (Shambhala Classics, rev. ed., 2010), another classic by Trungpa Rinpoche, covers the pitfalls of turning the spiritual path into a self-improvement project.

A Path with Heart: A Guide Through the Perils and Promises of Spiritual Life, by **Jack Kornfield** (Bantam, 1993): Classic work on meditation and how to integrate practice into everyday life, by one of the teachers who introduced Insight meditation to the West. Kornfield's *Meditation for Beginners* (Sounds True, 2008) gives step-by-step instructions for basic Buddhist practices and advice on cultivating a daily practice.

The Three Pillars of Zen, by **Roshi Philip Kapleau** (Anchor Books anniversary ed., 2013): Modern classic that introduced Westerners to Zen practice and *satori*—sudden enlightenment—by an influential Rinzai Zen master who was one of the first Americans to study Zen in a Japanese monastery and later founded the Rochester Zen Center.

What the Buddha Taught by **Walpola Rahula** (Grove, rev. ed., 2007): Indispensable volume on the essentials of Buddhism expressed clearly and in depth by a renowned Theravadan scholar-monk. A modern classic.

When Things Fall Apart: Heart Advice for Difficult Times, by **Pema Chödrön** (Shambhala, anniversary ed., 2016): Radical advice for navigating life's chaos from a popular American-born Tibetan Buddhist nun. For more of Ani Pema's practical wisdom, try *The Places That Scare You: A Guide to Fearlessness in Difficult Times* (Shambhala Classics, 2002); *Start Where You Are: A Guide to Compassionate Living* (Shambhala Library, 2004); and *Taking the Leap: Freeing Ourselves from Old Habits and Fears* (Shambhala, 2010).

Wherever You Go, There You Are: Mindfulness Meditation in Daily Life, by **Jon Kabat-Zinn** (Hachette Books, 10th ed., 2005): Amazon's bestselling Buddhist book. The author is a celebrated mindfulness teacher and stress researcher who created Mindfulness-Based Stress Reduction (MBSR). *Mindfulness for Beginners: Reclaiming the Present Moment and Your Life* (Sounds True, reprint ed., 2016) includes a CD with five guided meditations. Kabat-Zinn's *Falling Awake: How to Practice Mindfulness in Everyday Life* (Hachette Books, 2018) offers further teachings and practices on mindfulness.

Zen Flesh, Zen Bones: A Collection of Zen and Pre-Zen Writings, by Paul Reps and **Nyogen Senzaki** (Tuttle, 1998): Author Daniel Goleman, Dharma teacher Sylvia Boorstein, and basketball coach Phil Jackson are among the "millions" who claim this book was their introduction to Buddhism. Mindfulness maven Jon Kabat-Zinn says it provides "at the very least a glimpse of Zen mind at play in all its thought-shattering dialogue, humor, joy, and wisdom."

Zen Mind, Beginner's Mind, by **Shunryu Suzuki** (Shambhala, anniversary ed., 2011): If you buy only one Buddhist book, consider this one, drawn from Dharma talks by the most notable Zen master to arrive in America from Japan. The opening sentence—"In the beginner's mind there are many possibilities, but in the expert's there are few"—sets the tone for concise Dharma teachings delivered in Suzuki's singular, limpid style.

Meditation Seating

Meditators generally sit on a cushion on the floor, or if that's too difficult, on a chair or a meditation bench. Cushions come in a few standard shapes and sizes, although the covers and stuffing may vary. For tips on choosing the right cushion for the sitting posture you favor, see "How to Choose a Meditation Cushion" (sagemeditation.com/how-to-choose-a-meditation -cushion/).

Some sources for cushions:
Dakini Meditative (dakinimeditative.com/#cushions): Cushions, plus meditation courses and retreats
DharmaCrafts (dharmacrafts.com/00_cu/meditation-cushions)
Gaiam (gaiam.com/collections/meditation-seating)
Samaya (samaya.life)
Yoga Outlet (yogaoutlet.com/meditation-cushions-c11265)

Meditation benches come in a variety of styles. Among them:

Alexia Meditation Seat (alexiameditationseat.com): At the other extreme is the space-age Alexia. An ergonomically correct chair for proper meditation posture, it resembles a huge bird poised to take flight. Available in designer fabrics and colors, the Alexia has a small but loyal following among those who don't mind the hefty size, hefty price tag, and unusual shape.

Catizone Omni Meditation Bench (catizone.com): The Maserati of meditation benches, this is a sleek classic design in cherry. Has a round base for positional adjustment and spinal alignment, and folding legs for portability.

BackJack Chair (bjindustriesinc.com/backjack-chairs.htm): Another classic, a folding floor chair with a back and cushioned seat upholstered in duck canvas. Available in three sizes and nine colors.

Simply Sitting (simplysitting.com): A simple wooden kneeling bench shaped like a mushroom. Folds flat for carrying.

Index

About the Author

Emily Boland

JOHN DUNCAN OLIVER is a contributing editor at *Tricycle: The Buddhist Review* and an award-winning journalist whose work has appeared in such publications as *The New York Times, O, The Oprah Magazine, Health, Shambhala Sun, People, Self,* and *The Best Buddhist Writing 2005*. Her previous books include *Happiness, Good Karma, Coffee with the Buddha, The Meaning of Nice,* and *Commit to Sit,* an anthology of articles from *Tricycle*.

A Buddhist practitioner for forty years, she has studied with teachers from the Zen, Vipassana, and Tibetan Buddhist traditions, and from *Bön,* Tibet's oldest spiritual tradition.